Routledge Revivals

The Defeat of Debt

Prior to World War I, international trade was conducted based on what is known as the classical gold standard. In this system, trade between nations was settled using physical gold. Nations with trade surpluses accumulated gold as payment for their exports. Conversely, nations with trade deficits saw their gold reserves decline as gold flowed out of those nations as payment for their imports, creating debt laden economies, particularly for those countries impacted industrially by the First World War. In 1934, President Roosevelt signed the Gold Reserve Act which transferred the title of gold from private holders to the U.S. Treasury. The legislation successfully stopped the outflow of gold during the Great Depression. Originally published in 1935 this book discusses Roosevelt's actions and their consequences for the world economy as well as global democracy.

The Defeat of Debt

A Full Account of The Destruction of the Power of International Finance

R. McNair Wilson

Routledge
Taylor & Francis Group

First published in 1935 by George Routledge & Sons Ltd.

This edition first published in 2025 by Routledge
4 Park Square, Milton Park, Abingdon, Oxon, OX14 4RN
and by Routledge
605 Third Avenue, New York, NY 10158.

Routledge is an imprint of the Taylor & Francis Group, an informa business

ISBN 13: 978-1-041-08026-8 (hbk)
ISBN 13: 978-1-003-64338-8 (ebk)
ISBN 13: 978-1-041-08037-4 (pbk)
Book DOI 10.4324/9781003643388

THE DEFEAT OF DEBT

Being an account of the world-wide and secret battle which, on June 6th, 1935, ended in the downfall of the International Money Power Together with certain forecasts about the prosperity which all men are now about to enjoy

By

R. McNAIR WILSON

AUTHOR OF
"PROMISE TO PAY"; "YOUNG MAN'S MONEY"
"THE MIND OF NAPOLEON"; "MONARCHY AND MONEY POWER"

LONDON
GEORGE ROUTLEDGE & SONS, LTD.
BROADWAY HOUSE: 68–74 CARTER LANE, E.C.
1935

Printed in Great Britain by Butler & Tanner Ltd., Frome and London

To

ARTHUR KITSON

PIONEER AND FATHER
OF
ENGLISH MONETARY REFORM
AN ARCHITECT OF VICTORY

by whose courage, unselfishness and dogged perseverance in the cause of truth a foundation of knowledge was provided which nothing has been able to shake.

IN HOMAGE AND AFFECTION

CONTENTS

CONTENTS

CONCLUSION

PREFACE

On Thursday, June 6th, 1935, about midnight, a world-order, greater in strength than Imperial Rome, fell in irreparable defeat. The event passed almost unnoticed. This book is an attempt to bring it to notice.

In offering my book to the public I find myself in the difficulty of making suitable acknowledgment to the large body of workers in the field covered by it upon whose thought and argument I have so freely drawn. I have dedicated the book to Mr. Arthur Kitson because it is upon the pioneer work of such as he that the triumph of June 6th is based. No man has ever enjoyed a prouder distinction among his fellows. I wish, in this as in earlier works, to express my indebtedness to the Rev. S. N. L. Ford, Vicar of All Souls', Loudoun Road, London. Mr. Ford's views are embodied in this book; the clearness of his thinking and the courage of his expression have been of inestimable value to many in these difficult days. Again, I must thank Mr. Featherstone Hammond for the help he has given me in so many different ways. Mr. Hammond's own writings attest his knowledge and deserve careful study. Some of them have appeared in *G.K.'s Weekly* which is, to-day, the best informed of the weeklies about the undercurrents of finance and politics and which, consequently, has become indispensable to the serious student. I should like, further, to offer my thanks to Mr. Christopher Hollis who has already, in *The Breakdown of Money*, struck a shrewd blow and who is now about to strike another in *The Two Nations*.

No writer upon this subject can omit reference to the fundamental contributions made to it by Professor Soddy of Oxford. Professor Soddy has paid tribute to help given him by Mr. Kitson.

To my publisher, Mr. Fredric Warburg, I wish to offer the thanks of an author who has received both encouragement and help.

I wish above all to thank my dear wife for a tolerance which seems to be without limit. I have covered the walls of our house with innumerable charts and maps and plans and littered it with cuttings. She has made comment only to say that all these add to the liveliness of decoration.

R. McNAIR WILSON.

LONDON.

July 14*th*, 1935.

THE DEFEAT OF DEBT

INTRODUCTION

In the course of his annual address for 1935, the Chairman of the Cunard Company expressed the view that a war, unacknowledged and secret, but not the less on that account violent and disastrous, was being waged in every corner of the world. Sir Percy Bates did not offer any exact description of this war, but he spoke in anxious tones about the restrictions upon trade and upon exchange which, as he said, were attending its progress.

It is probable that few of those who heard him possessed any clear idea of his meaning. It is probable, too, that the majority of that particular audience felt convinced that the war if it existed would be won, as usual, by those powers upon whom, as upon its pillars, the structure of modern society reposes. In fact, however, victory has gone to the enemies of those powers so that, suddenly, and unexpectedly, humanity has come to a crisis of its history.

It is the purpose of the pages which follow to give an account of the secret war, to describe its origins and chief events and to discover the manner of its ending so that the nature of the crisis now existing may be understood. The world into which all now living were born must speedily pass away and will not return. A new world, and a new social structure, will arise in its place.

The question: " Of what nature is this new world likely to be ? " cannot, evidently, be answered unless the character and aims of the victors in the secret war are known, for it is they who will be the chief architects of the future. Nor can it be answered if there is lacking a clear understanding of the foundations upon which the old world reposed. Wars break out when the possibility of compromise no longer exists because the aim of one of the parties must, if realized, destroy the other party. The secret war furnished no exception to this rule. An element necessary to the life of the existing social organism was being denied to the organism. There was no choice but to give battle immediately, with all available forces. The nature of this element is, thus, the key to understanding not only of the form which the Society of to-morrow will assume but also of the foundations upon which it is likely to rest.

The element in question is debt. The social organism, which has just been destroyed, was nourished and sustained by the borrowing and lending of money and could not, therefore, exist at all in a debtless world. It has fallen fighting for debt against those who desire to abolish debt from the earth. Its growth corresponded strictly with the growth of debt in European countries, and the process of its growth was characterized by the same kind of warfare as that which has attended its downfall. For the growth of debt was not less hurtful to the social organism which existed formerly than has been the decline of debt to this social organism. The Debt System triumphed because its practitioners found a fresh source of lendable money; it has been vanquished because its enemies devised means of converting that source to their own uses.

It cannot be understood too clearly that circumstances of recurring depression in agriculture and industry, that is to say of poverty, are necessary to the practice of moneylending, since, in the continued absence of poverty, men tend to get out of debt. Depression, for all practical purposes, means a fall in the level of prices. Unless, therefore, moneylenders can exert control of price-levels they are bound, sooner or later, to go out of business from want of borrowers. An absolute control of prices was achieved when, early in the last century, the world was persuaded to accept and use the promissory notes of bankers as its money instead of gold and silver.[1] A banker's signature belongs to himself and cannot, without forgery, be reproduced by anybody else. If, therefore, he chooses to remove his signature-money from the world's markets all prices in these markets are bound to collapse.

Nor was there remedy against that catastrophe. In

[1] These promises to pay were originally receipts for cash deposited with the bankers. People began to use the receipts instead of money. Bankers now issued receipts without any backing of cash and so increased the supply of money ten or more times. All this new " money " was issued in the form of loans.

earlier times, when a scarcity of gold or silver money had threatened the stability of prices, Kings had not hesitated to melt down their coinages and, of one coin, to make, by alloying or other device, two or even three new ones. But a signature cannot be melted or alloyed, or multiplied.

It is, even now, very imperfectly understood how great was the power conferred upon bankers by the Credit, that is to say the Debt, System. He who has persuaded his fellows to employ his signature instead of money and who has made it impossible for them to obtain any other kind of money has become their master. If he issues his signature in the form of loans he puts the world, immediately, in his debt to the extent of the whole of its means of exchange. And what he has lent he can take back again. When he chooses, the transfer of goods from seller to buyer can be prevented, crops left to rot in the fields, machinery caused to stand idle, men and women rendered destitute and governments bankrupted.

The practitioners of the Debt System were accustomed, at the first whisper of resistance, to protect their power by withdrawing their money. So terrible were the consequences to their fellows of this withdrawal that even the strongest governments capitulated as a rule immediately. Indeed, the threat of withdrawal was enough, usually, to induce an attitude of submission.

In these circumstances the fact that the Secret War against the Debt System has convulsed the world cannot be looked upon as matter of surprise. In such a war the world was bound to be convulsed seeing that destruction and desolation are the invariable concomitants of a sudden withdrawal of the means of exchange. What is surprising, however, is the escape of the world from that chaos which the masters of Debt so confidently predicted as the inevitable result of any attack upon their system. It would seem that there lives in the hearts of men a faith stronger than the forces of disintegration and despair. That faith has been the architect of victory. Upon its sure foundation the pillars of the New World will rest.

BOOK I

CASUS BELLI

CHAPTER I

ENGLAND REJECTS

THE statement has often been made that the year of the Diamond Jubilee of Queen Victoria, 1897, marked the zenith of British power and prestige. It marked at the same time a low ebb of the level of prices in Great Britain and throughout the world. Prices had been falling since the Battle of Waterloo, eighty-two years before; they had fallen with an occasional, temporary rise, steadily and continuously. Belief was general that the fall would go on.

That belief was called Progress; for it was everywhere held that falling prices are the necessary foundation of a rising standard of living. British power, it was asserted, had been built upon falling prices which, alone, had enabled British statesmen to carry out the policies of reform that were the envy of the world. In consequence there was nothing but admiration for a system which secured that prices should continue to fall. Next to his Parliament, in order of merit, the Englishman of the year 1897 placed his monetary system.

It would have surprised him, therefore, had he been told that, as originally conceived, his monetary system, the Gold Standard, was designed not to cause prices to fall but to keep them stable. The Gold Standard in these latter days, has few defenders ; this is unfair because the Gold Standard has never yet, anywhere, been put into operation. It was meant to regulate, automatically, the quantity of money in the markets so that an average level of prices might be maintained from one year to another. If prices should tend to rise the Gold Standard regulator, it was believed, would cut off the supply of money, that is to say of buyers. If, on the contrary, prices should tend to fall the supply of money would be increased. The means by which this automatic action was to be secured were simple : buyers all over the world were to be free to go into any market they chose. High prices at home, when the money of one country can be exchanged without loss for the monies of all other countries, send buyers into foreign markets and so cause prices at home to fall ; low prices at home attract foreign buyers and so cause prices at home to rise.

The Gold Standard was the interpreter between the national monies. The pound sterling, the dollar, the franc, the mark, the lira could all be exchanged for a fixed quantity of gold ; all consequently maintained a fixed relationship with one another. All price-levels, therefore, would have been the same throughout the world and would have remained the same if the International Gold Standard had been allowed to work automatically. The fact that, on the contrary, all price-levels fell after the standard had been established, is proof that its automatic working was hindered. The standard was allowed to lower prices when they had risen but was not allowed to raise them again when they had fallen.

The device by which the automatic working of the Gold Standard was prevented was the foreign loan. It is obvious that if the money which foreign buyers bring to a low-price market is instantly taken away from that market and lent to some distant country, the effect upon prices of the increase in the number of buyers will be cancelled out. The loan will take away as much money as the foreign buyers are bringing in and no change in the level of prices will occur. When it is recalled that England alone lent abroad some £7,000,000,000 during the final quarter of the Nineteenth Century the extent to which the automatic working of the Gold Standard was tampered with can be realized. All the creditor nations practised what was, in truth, a policy of hoarding by lending. The Gold Standard was transformed, in consequence, from a mechanism designed to give the world the blessing of stable prices into a mechanism which, infallibly, lowered the prices of every country to the level of the cheapest country—that is to say to the level of the country where wages were smallest and the conditions of life and work least satisfactory.

Some vague uneasiness occasioned by this misuse of an excellent mechanism had entered the minds of a few British statesmen on the day when the cream ponies drew the royal coach through London. For Progress tarried and poverty was everywhere in evidence. One of these statesmen was Mr. Joseph Chamberlain, in whose mind proposals for Empire Trade and protective tariffs were beginning to form. During the ten years which followed the Diamond Jubilee, England, thanks to Mr. Chamberlain, was divided on the Free Trade issue; but among the upholders of Free Trade was the author of the National Insurance Act with its provision for Unemployment Benefit, "the dole".

It was easy, thirty years ago, to see the difference between the policy of Mr. Chamberlain and that of Mr. Lloyd George. Was not the former a Unionist and the latter a Liberal? To-day the distinction is less obvious; "Tariff Reform" and the "Dole" both tend to prevent an outflow of buying-power from home markets into foreign markets. In the case of the tariff, the effect is exerted upon buying-power directly; in the case of the dole it is exerted upon wages which are hindered from falling; but as wages, in every country, constitute the body and bulk of buying-power, the difference is unimportant. In the retrospect it is clear that the two ablest and most popular statesmen in Great Britain were simultaneously, and from opposing platforms, advocating policies inimical to foreign lending and were, in consequence, making a stand against those who, by foreign loans, had defeated the automatic working of the International Gold Standard.

An immense confusion surrounds this subject and it is necessary, therefore, to insist once more that the original object of the Gold Standard was the stabilization of prices and that the actual effect of the Gold Standard—namely, a continuous fall of prices—was brought about by tampering with its automatic working. Mr. Chamberlain and Mr. Lloyd George were champions of the Gold Standard as originally conceived, even though, as is probable, they were unaware of the implications of their policies. They were "stable-money" men; supporters of a "commodity pound", which, from year to year and from generation to generation, should buy the same average quantity of goods, neither more nor less.

They encountered, consequently, from the beginning, the opposition of those who, by foreign lending, were preventing the stabilization of prices. Thanks to that opposition the Conservative Party was split and later brought to defeat in the General Election of 1906, while a similar split, the real cause of which was obscured by the Great War, divided the Liberal Party and brought it to ruin—but not before the principle of unemployment insurance had been accepted by the country. Great Britain, in other words, followed its chosen leaders, declared for stable prices against falling prices, and thus rejected the doctrine of "continuous fall" which had been the gospel of the Nineteenth Century.

It does not signify that this rejection was instinctive rather than conscious. Men voted for unemployment insurance because they were sorry for the unemployed and ashamed of a system which produced unemployment. Few men, probably, realized that a "dole" sets limits to the reduction which can be effected in the level of wages; but such realization, if it had occurred would not, in all likelihood, have affected the result of the voting. Again, the number of persons who knew anything about the effect of irreducible wages on costs of production and so on prices was very small, but there is nothing to show that, had it been very large, the system of unemployment insurance would have been rejected. Finally, had the British people understood that they were striking a blow for stable prices the blow would not, probably, on that account, have lost its force.

All this was understood clearly in the money markets of the world. In these money markets the simple truth was never forgotten that, when prices are stable, people get out of debt and that consequently any and every attempt to keep prices stable is a threat to the Credit, or Debt, system. The Debt System had marched like an army across Europe : from Florence to Venice and Genoa ; from Venice and Genoa to Geneva and Amsterdam and Frankfort-on-the-Maine ; from Geneva and Amsterdam and Frankfort-on-the-Maine to London. Once more the tents were unpegged and folded. While the dogs barked, the caravan made ready to pass on from London, across the Atlantic, to New York, where the idea of insurance for the unemployed did not find favour, and where, incidentally, there was no impending threat of German invasion.

The years which followed witnessed the preparation of New York to become the financial centre of the world. America possessed a tariff ; she did not possess a central bank. It was necessary to get rid of the one and to establish the other. It was necessary, further, to stamp out from the American mind, all hankerings after a bi-metallic standard seeing that the foreign loan Gold Standard is hindered in its operation if silver can take the place of gold and so prevent a fall of prices. In the year 1900 the United States Congress passed the Gold Standard Act and made an end, finally, of silver as a basis of money. In 1907 a financial panic in New York and elsewhere led to an active demand for banking "reform". A monetary Commission was set up and a bill for the establishing of a central bank was introduced into Congress, where, however, it was defeated in 1911. Two years later, on December 20th, 1913, the Federal Reserve Bill, by which a Central Banking System of a somewhat complicated kind was inaugurated, became the law of the land. The Great War began seven months later on August 4th, 1914. Its chief effect, in the economic sphere, was the elevation of America to the position of the world's creditor and consequently the transference of the world's gold stock from London to New York.

The coming of President Woodrow Wilson to the Peace Conference at Versailles partook, in the circumstances, of a triumphal progress. Was he not the Chief-of-State of the country, which, as the world's creditor, now held the world's supply of gold [1] and which, in consequence, was become the headquarters of the Debt System? But the triumph soon ended when the American people learned that they were being brought into the League of Nations and committed to courses which must, sooner or later, entail the reduction or removal of the American tariff. Mr. Wilson lost the whole of his popularity. His signature upon

[1] This gold was, of course, privately owned by the masters of money.

the Peace Treaty was repudiated by Congress which, under the compulsion of its constituents, declared that the tariff would not be removed or reduced. America, in other words, rejected the Debt System by refusing, flatly, to establish the conditions necessary to the functioning of that system. Like England she declared for stable prices against falling prices under the guidance of an instinct which was not the less sound because it lacked support in technical knowledge.

The Dealers in Debt now found themselves in a sad predicament. They were faced with the lively danger that America, the world's creditor, might employ the Gold Standard in the manner in which the authors of that standard had intended that it should be employed. Terrible prospects of a stable price-level and a debt-less world drove them to action. Every resource which money is able to command was mobilized immediately against the American people.

CHAPTER II

COLLAPSE

THE American tariff denied to American buyers free access to low-price European markets. It prevented, in consequence, a fall in American prices, and so, to some extent, in prices throughout the world, for most of the countries of the world were then as they are now, large buyers of American goods and raw materials. The main attack of the Masters of the Debt System was directed, therefore, against the tariff.

How could the American people be induced to suspend its tariff? The answer was obvious: by being induced, in the first instance, to invest in foreign loans, the interest upon which could be paid only in goods. Let the investors discover that payment of monies due to them was being made impossible by the tariff and their support of the tariff would determine.

Foreign lending, however, was out of the question while all the countries of the world, except America, remained off the foreign-loan Gold Standard. The world had to be helped back to that standard, therefore, before any steps could be taken. A more formidable task has seldom confronted desperate men. For those countries which were most eager to borrow from America were the least credit-worthy. Germany is the outstanding example. Loaded with debts and reparations, that defeated and humiliated people was incapable, without substantial help, of linking its inflated currency to gold. The Masters of Money appealed to government after government to extend forgiveness to the beaten foe; but no government dared, in this matter, to act alone. As the year 1922 drew to a close it became apparent that the destruction of the mark was the indispensable prerequisite of the stabilization of that currency. Destruction, in fact, took place during the following year. In 1924 the mark returned to a gold basis at 0·0000000001 per cent of its pre-war value. The Austrian schilling had already been stabilized at 0·00007 per cent. These movements are shown in Fig. 1, which gives a rapid survey of the course of events.

All the governments of the world now engaged in a race back to the foreign-loan Gold Standard in order to be qualified as recipients of American bounty. England, Holland, Denmark and Switzerland stabilized at 100 per cent, Finland at 13 per cent, Hungary at 0·0069 per cent, Belgium at 14·5 per cent, Italy at 27·3 per cent, Poland at 0·000026 per cent and France at 20·3 per cent. In addition England settled her War Debt with America, promising to pay some £15,000,000 half-yearly for 60 years. Lending to Germany and other countries by Americans began immediately on a scale without precedent in the history of the world. During 1924, Germany imported $400,000,000. In 1925 she imported $850,000,000, in 1927 $1,050,000,000 and in 1928 $1,000,000,000. The question: "How is

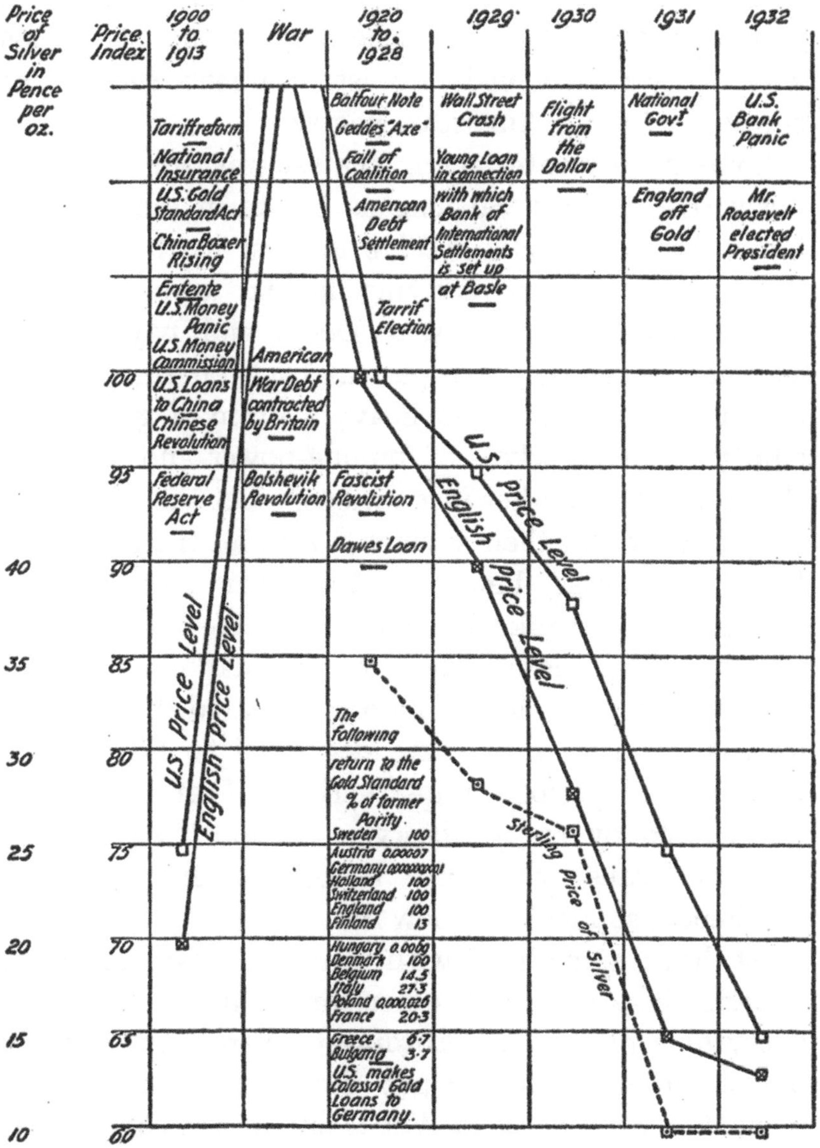

FIG. 1.—THE SLUMP.
1920–1928 = 100.

America to receive the interest on this colossal sum of money?" was asked everywhere by instructed persons who had watched, in lively astonishment, the sale of the loans to the American people.

Some at any rate among the salesmen of the loans knew the answer: So long as her tariff remained in force, America would receive interest in the form of gold just as she was receiving, in that form, payment of the instalments of War Debts and payment of commercial debts. Europe was back on the foreign-loan Gold Standard; so heavy a drain of gold must empty all her markets of buying-power and threaten the stability of all her institutions. Let the American investors look to their savings. And let the American farmers, likewise, beware. More than half of their cotton crop—to take but one example—must be sold every year in those ruined foreign markets.

The Masters of Money, having prepared these object lessons, awaited with some degree of confidence the issue of the period of instruction. That confidence was shared by many observers, so much so, indeed, that the cause of Tariff Reform in England was quickened, suddenly, to new life. England, it was felt, must have something with which to bargain when America began to remove her trade barriers. In fact, everything proceeded according to plan. The outflow of gold from Europe to pay the interest on the new loans, the instalments of War Debt and the commercial debts reduced European buying-power by some 40 per cent and so brought down the prices of all goods but especially of farm goods, the production of which cannot be reduced as quickly as the production of factory goods. The American farmer began to get less for his wheat, his cotton and his sugar, while unsold surpluses choked the home market and exerted their influence on the price pattern, that is to say the relationship between the prices of farm goods and the prices of factory goods.

During all this time the general level of prices in America had remained stable, thanks to the tariff and

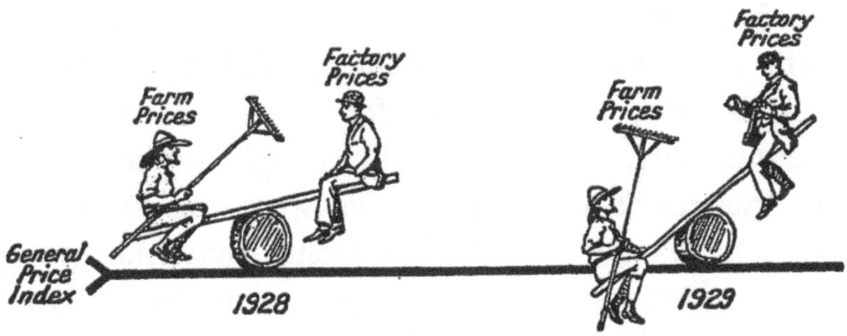

FIG. 2.—THE CAUSE OF THE AMERICAN BOOM.
Note that the general level of prices remained unaffected.

to the determination of Congress. But such a general level is always a see-saw with the farmer seated on one end and the factory-owner on the other. If the farmer's prices fall the factory-owner's prices must rise so long as the see-saw remains in action—so long, that is to say, as the general average of all prices, the "level", remains constant. The accompanying figures (Fig. 2) show this see-saw action. They show how the factory prices rose while the farm prices fell and they explain why the great boom on Wall Street took place. The boom was based on the rising prices of factory goods and on the increased earnings of industrial companies. But since factories exist by selling their products to farmers and since the farmers of America were in process of ruin, the end of the boom was certain. Sooner or later factory prices must break and the general level of prices, the entire see-saw, collapse.

Collapse took place in the autumn of the year 1929 when the great " Wall Street crash " shook the structure of business throughout the world. Farm and factory shared, now, the same ruin not in America only but universally.

The event supplied the Masters of Money, who were its architects, with a text for a tidy homily about economic law. The American people replied that if the price-levels of all countries were the same there would be no need for tariffs seeing that men buy in foreign markets only when prices in these foreign markets are lower than prices at home. This was of course, a restatement of the case for the automatic Gold Standard. Had the Masters of Money been seized with a passion for candour they might have pointed out that stable prices and the Debt System cannot long be bedfellows and that, consequently, moneylenders can never give support to a policy of price stabilization.

In fact, the Masters of Money felt sure of victory. Though gold was the basis of money, the money based upon the gold consisted of their promises to pay, that is to say of their signatures, and there was no other kind of money in the world. Further, all this private-signature-money had been issued in the form of loans; all of it was, therefore, debt owned by the peoples of the world to the Masters of Money. The weakness of the American people, as of all other peoples, lay in the circumstance that its money consisted of debt-money. It was that fact which had made the refusal of America to remove her tariff a whip for America's back. As has been said the tariff, by preventing the entry of goods, caused a drain of gold from Europe. Each piece of gold, while in Europe, had carried on its back, so to speak, ten private promises to pay it—ten pieces of private-"credit"-money lent to Europeans. The banker who had made these ten promises necessarily cancelled them at once when the piece of gold on which they were based passed out of his hands—in other words he called in the loan and so took buying-power out of the market. Had any source of money other than private-signature-money existed this calamitous destruction of buying-power need not have occurred because the ten pieces of private-signature-money would in that case immediately have been replaced from the alternative source.

If, for example, the various governments of Europe had been in a position to buy silver with their own signatures then government-signature-money would have gone out into the markets to replace the private-signature-money and the newly purchased silver would have gone into the vaults of the Government as backing for the issue. The drain of gold to America would not, in these circumstances, have caused a fall of European and so, later, of American prices. Unhappily all governments were bound by laws which forbade them to use more than a trifling quantity of silver as backing for signature-money issued by them. Again, governments might have used their own signatures to pay debts and so to put government-signature-money into circulation without any metallic backing. But here, too, the law barred the way by insisting that every piece of government-signature-money must possess a backing of metal.

These laws prevented effectually the replacing of private-signature-money by government-signature-money and stand as proof that all the governments of the world (which made the laws) obeyed the dictates of the Masters of Money. The spectacle of an apparently powerful government in paralysis for want of the signatures of a few of its private citizens is similar to the spectacle of a rabbit being hounded to death by a stoat. Can the signature of a private person who, on his own showing, is promising to pay ten times the quantity of legal tender money in his possession be of greater worth than the signature of a government possessed of the taxable income of a nation? The conclusion is unavoidable that the world's governments, though elected by popular vote, are controlled by the Masters of Money either through the ignorance or through the cowardice of the leaders of these governments. The government reigns but does not govern.

The American farmers were the first victims of the fall of European prices. They suffered, but did not demand the removal of the tariff, thus signally disappointing the hopes of the Masters of Money. The American factory workers proved no less obdurate when their turn came to suffer. But it was different in the case of the American investor who had bought the German and other loans. As soon as the investor became aware that Germany had no more gold to send in payment of interest, he began, as anticipated, to demand the cancellation of War Debts and the removal of the tariff.

America was now divided into two warring camps: namely, the farmers and workers and the investors and bankers. Small business belonged to the former group, big business to the latter. Meanwhile the Masters of Money, throughout the world, were growing a little uneasy. They had prepared and launched a major attack which had succeeded so well that there was scarcely a solvent business, farm or factory, left in America; but the enemy had not been driven from his position. The tariff remained and the drain of gold from Europe continued. Would the weapon they had forged become a boomerang to strike at themselves?

CHAPTER III

THE PRICE OF GOLD

THE circumstances attending the collapse in America deserve the careful attention of Englishmen. Had the collapse produced the effect aimed at—namely the removal of the American tariff—Wall Street would have begun at once to play the part which Lombard Street had played during the Nineteenth Century. Loans would have been made to every country willing to accept them and able to offer reasonable security.

The effect, if the experience of the Nineteenth Century is a guide, must have been the re-grouping of debtor nations, round New York instead of round London. These debtor nations would have included members of the British Commonwealth and the fact that British Dominions had become dependent for supplies of money upon Wall Street would, sooner or later, have brought about the disintegration of the British Empire however much the Dominions themselves might have resisted that tendency.

It must not be inferred from this, however, that the only links of Empire are financial links. The British Empire is based not upon money but upon a common loyalty. It is a spiritual unity that has been harmed rather than helped by the fact that most of the Dominions are debtors to the Mother Country. In a world, however, where the only money available is the private-signature-money of international bankers, debtor countries must set their necessity against their feelings. Had the Masters of Money succeeded in making New York the financial centre of the world, every borrower would have been compelled to go to New York just as, during the Nineteenth Century, every borrower was compelled to come to London. New York and her Money Masters in consequence would have possessed the power to bend English policy to their desire.

It is when this truth is realized and understood that the service rendered by the American people to the English people becomes clear. Not British statesmen nor British bankers but American farmers and workers saved the British Empire from what was, probably, the most serious danger that has ever threatened it—the Great War not excluded. Most British statesmen, so far as their ideas can be gleaned from their speeches, seem to have swallowed whole the propaganda of the Masters of Money against the American tariff and British bankers displayed no greater acumen. It is difficult to find anywhere, even in the mouths of the most perfervid Tariff Reformers, tribute to the courage displayed by the American people in defending their level of prices and their standard of living and, incidentally, in preventing the Masters of the Debt System from reducing England to the status of a small island.

Nor does it signify if the American people acted

without the least idea of what they were doing. Every student of history learns, early in his career, that great events proceed as a rule from instincts and impulses rather than from conscious processes of reason. The English rejection of Money Power, as has been suggested, was instinctive rather than deliberate; the American rejection was of the same quality. In neither case were parliaments the originators of resistance. Resistance came up, rather, from humble homes.

In America it was resistance of so stubborn and refractory a character as to break the greatest assault which Money Power had, until then, launched against mankind. On the morrow of the Wall Street crash, the Masters of Money found themselves as far from their goal as they had been when the prosperity of America was the wonder of the world. And this although they had wrecked what they were pleased to describe as civilization. Anxiously they drew off their forces for reformation.

It was obvious, now, that many of the countries which had been brought back with so much labour to the foreign-loan Gold Standard would abandon that standard once more. There is, perhaps, no limit to human endurance; but a definite limit is set to any fall in prices—namely, the point at which the securities lodged with banks in exchange for their loans become unsaleable at a price high enough to enable the bank to recover the amount of its loan. When that point has been reached one of two things happens: either the outflow of gold is stopped by decree or the relationship with gold is severed so that it is no longer necessary to call up loans when gold leaves the country. The continued existence of the American tariff made it certain that gold would go on flowing to New York.

The Masters of Money, therefore, prepared for the inevitable and so contrived that, when the blow fell, it should strike their enemies and not themselves. They foresaw, for example, that England would be driven off gold and they knew that, when this happened, London would be forced to maintain a free market for the metal. The English price of gold, in other words, would be determined by supply and demand and would, consequently, be capable of movement up or down according as demand exceeded supply or supply demand. Further, it would be possible to buy and sell gold "forward", because merchants would require the safeguard, in troublous times, of a future market in the metal.

In other words, the Masters of Money saw their way clear, by buying and selling, to exert influence upon the sterling price of gold, and so, if America remained on the Gold Standard, to force down still further her already sorely depressed level of prices.

The mechanism of this operation is simple: International prices are gold prices; if, therefore, the dollar "contains" more gold than the pound, dollar goods will be dearer in foreign markets than pound goods. American goods, for example, which are on sale in Paris are priced not in dollars but in francs. If the goods cost, say, $10 to make and if the dollar is worth 15 francs, then the price must be 150 francs. If, on the contrary, the dollar is worth only 10 francs then the price would be 100 francs. The value of dollars and of francs depends on the quantity of gold which these monies will buy—on their "gold content". If the dollar price of gold rises, then each dollar will contain less gold and be worth fewer francs; if, on the other hand, the dollar price of gold falls then each dollar will contain more gold and be worth more francs. The effect, consequently, of raising the pound price of gold is to make the pound worth fewer dollars or francs, so long as the amount of gold in these currencies remains unchanged, so long, that is to say, as America and France remain on the Gold Standard at existing levels.

The Masters of Money were, naturally, very well equipped for buying or selling gold—they were the Masters of Money. If they desired that the pound price of gold should rise, who was to oppose them? It is not easy for a poor man to outbid those to whom the whole universe is in debt.

On September 21st, 1931, England was forced to abandon the Gold Standard. The sterling price of gold immediately rose sharply and the pound became worth fewer dollars. In consequence, English merchants were able to sell their goods in foreign markets at lower prices than had been possible before the break with gold. Further those countries of the British Empire and those foreign countries which abandoned the Gold Standard at the same time as England obtained the same advantage. The American manufacturer and the American farmer were faced with a new and very severe form of competition, which promised, unless America also abandoned the Gold Standard, to prove almost as severe a chastisement as the original collapse of prices. America did not abandon the Gold Standard. Instead she tried to reduce the prices of her goods by making drastic cuts in wages and in public expenditure. The effect is shown in Fig. 3.

The occasion was improved by the usual homilies from the Masters of Money. If, they said, the American tariff had been removed the great collapse in prices would not have taken place. England, consequently, would not have been forced to abandon the Gold Standard and her Dominions and India would not, therefore, have been able to undersell American wheat, cotton and sugar in the world's markets. The American farmer would not have been brought to beggary and the American employer of labour would not have been compelled to cut his wages or discharge his men.

It was all true. But it was true, also, that if America had removed her tariff her people would have fallen into the hands of the Masters of Money to be used, for ever, as "industrial cannon fodder".

Throughout the bitter months of the year 1932 the sterling price of gold continued its rise with an occasional interruption; throughout that year the American price-level went on falling, as did also the price-levels of France, Italy, Germany and other states. Buying-power, everywhere, was shrinking from day to day and week to week, and, as it shrank, fresh desperate efforts to cut wages and prices were made in every country.

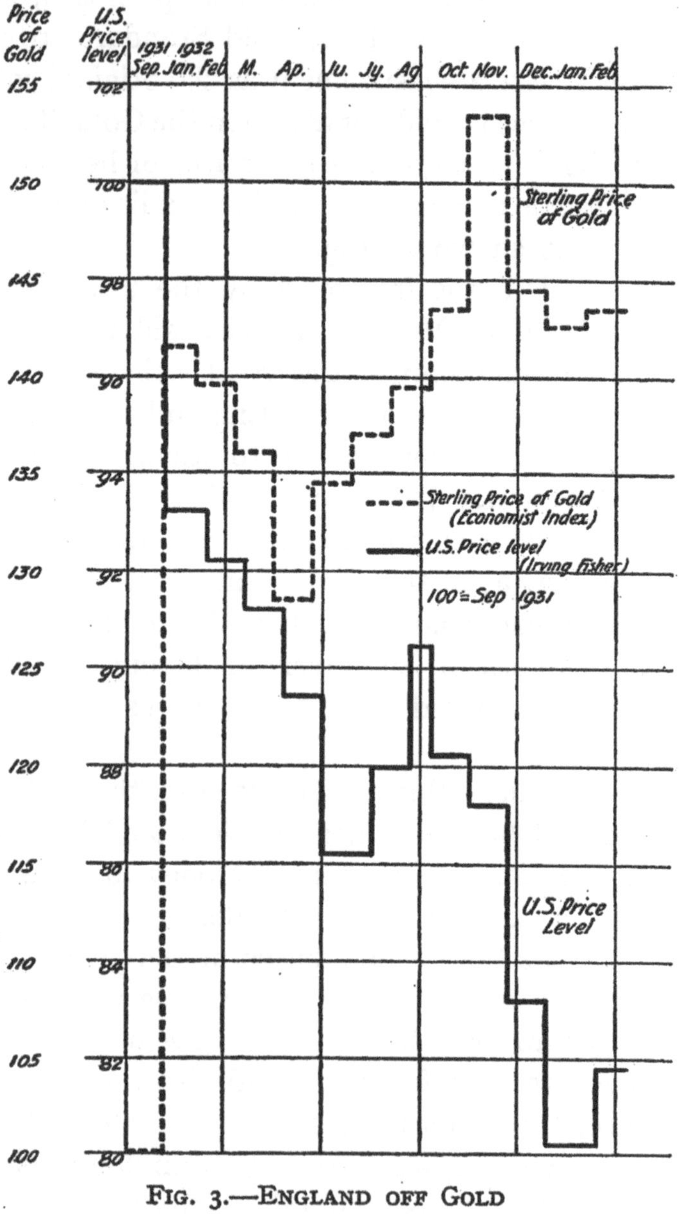

FIG. 3.—ENGLAND OFF GOLD
Effect of rise in sterling price of gold on U.S. price-level.

An astonished world beheld the spectacle of " Poverty amid Plenty " and men asked themselves, anxiously, why goods that so many desired and needed had to be burnt like rubbish or cast, like offal, into the sea. Few, probably, who asked these questions, knew that a life-and-death struggle, a great war to the knife, was being waged at their doors between the two strongest forces in the world—Man and Money. The Masters of Money, far from seeking a way out of the crisis, were exerting themselves in every corner of the earth to increase its severity. Everywhere they were calling up loans and destroying money—that signature-money of theirs which could not be replaced. Everywhere they were gathering food-stuffs and fabrics to fling them, in overwhelming mass, upon markets glutted already with these goods and destitute of the money necessary to buy them. As they laboured one thought only possessed their minds : the American people must break under this strain which is more than can be endured.

But the American people did not break. On the contrary, when the suspicion arose that President Hoover might be induced to declare a second moratorium for War Debt, an angry outburst warned him that his people was as vigilant and as determined as ever. The Masters of Money bought gold on the London Market in great quantities after that outburst and the pound price of the metal rose sharply, sending the American and Continental price-levels reeling down to new depths. But the tariff remained. And the time was approaching rapidly at which, if prices continued to fall, every bank in the United States would have to close its doors. The Masters of Money hardened their hearts. Let the banks close; that lesson, at any rate, could not fail to bring the most obdurate to a sense of reality.

CHAPTER IV

DARKEST HOUR

IT is often argued that the Masters of Money bear no responsibility for the catastrophe of America. How, for example, it is asked, could they have prevented the return by the world to the Gold Standard, which was the cause of the catastrophe? The answer is that Wall Street and other financial centres refused to make any loans to any countries which had not returned to the Gold Standard. At the end of the War, money was indispensable to the world's recovery; money could be obtained only from Wall Street and those other centres where the authors of private-signature-money ply their craft. The world had no option.

Again, it is asked why America should be pitied seeing that she herself was the architect of her own downfall? After all, it was she and none else who refused to take payment in goods and insisted upon being paid in gold. It must have been obvious to her statesmen that ruin would attend so selfish a demand. The answer is that, had she accepted payment in goods, by removing her tariff, her standard of living would inevitably have been reduced to that of the lowest-standard country. America was not trying, as is frequently alleged, to live to herself. She was trying to live. As in the case of England, a monetary system designed to force prices to lower and ever lower levels, had awakened a strong spirit of resistance. In the circumstances it is pertinent to inquire what would have happened had the world not been forced back to the foreign-loan Gold Standard while the wage-levels in Europe remained lower than the American wage-level.

America, in these circumstances, could not have obtained gold from her debtors because these debtors could not have converted their money into gold. Nor could she have obtained dollars, because dollar credits in European hands were few. She would, therefore, have been compelled to trade goods for goods or to cease to trade altogether. But, since Europe's need of American goods is much greater than America's need of European goods, Europe, at a barter conference, would have been forced to accept America's terms—namely, stabilized prices at the American level. It was the certainty of such an issue, if things were left to themselves, which caused the Masters of Money to insist upon a general return to gold.

Few people in England realize how great was the American interest in stabilized prices in the years preceding and immediately following the War. The Federal Reserve Act itself had a "stabilizing" clause, which, however, was struck out of it. Irving Fisher declared at the time: "My definition of a perfectly elastic currency would be one which varied with the demands of trade in such a manner as to maintain the price-level constant."

Resolution after resolution and bill after bill had

been introduced into Congress with the object of compelling the Federal Reserve System to keep the price-level stable and the level, in fact, remained stable from 1920 until 1929. During this time discussion of stabilization went on daily throughout the country. Seeing, as has been pointed out, and as is obvious, that stable prices deliver men from debt, the anxiety of the Masters of Debt is easily understood. They saw the country which they had chosen as the headquarters of their system and to which they had transferred so much of their wealth beginning to hanker after policies which threatened everything for which, and by which, they stood. And they saw, further, that, very soon, stabilization of prices would be forced upon Europe as the condition of trading with America.

It remains to ask whether, when the collapse of America had actually taken place, recovery could have been brought about at any time by the Masters of Money. Again the answer must lie against the Masters. They could have ended the crisis. When England left the Gold Standard, the situation which would have occurred had there been no return to gold—namely the cessation of trade between England and America—became once more a possibility. The Masters of Money, however, by buying gold on the London market, caused the price of the metal to rise sharply and so attracted to London the great hoards of India and the East. This new gold was disposed of to persons having debts to meet in America, so that the "drain of gold" to New York was not suffered to come to an end. In addition, as has been seen, the rising price of gold in London forced America and Europe to save what remained of their export trade by fresh cuts in prices. Had the policy of gold-buying been abandoned a conference with America about barter-buying ("Yankee Trading") would immediately have become necessary, and the English and American price-levels would have been stabilized—probably by means of the original, automatic Gold Standard.

The Masters of Money, therefore, did not object to the drain of gold to New York. On the contrary they brought it about, deliberately, by forcing the world back to the Gold Standard, and maintained it, after England had abandoned gold, by operations on the bullion markets which had the effect of further reducing the world's levels of prices. In these circumstances, the homilies against the selfishness of the American people are humbug, especially in view of what occurred in America during the winter of 1932–3.

During that winter, as has been seen, the American price-level reached a point at which the whole banking system of the country became insolvent. The securities held by the banks against their loans became worth less than the amounts of the loans. The question must, in these circumstances, have arisen whether or not the process of deflation should be eased; whether, in other words, the buying of gold should be reduced in volume. Buying of gold (as Fig. 3 shows) was not reduced in volume and the pressure on the American banks continued. All the American banks failed.

When banks begin to fail farmers refuse to bring food to the towns and townspeople starve. In such circumstances chaos is on the doorstep. The authority of government disappears and mob rule replaces the rule of constituted authority. There is then no sacrifice which is likely to be refused. Having failed to remove the American tariff by the collapse of 1929 and by the pressure of the rising sterling price of gold, the Masters of Money were about to try their hand at methods of starvation, panic, and disorder.

It is impossible to say whether or not they would have succeeded. During the long months of the darkest winter in human story, the American people had displayed an admirable resignation and a great courage. Its determination to uphold its national standards had not perceptibly weakened. On the other hand, the march of hunger could scarcely have been stayed if the financial system of the country had gone down in collapse, and hunger soon robs men of their self-control. Happily, the darkest hour had discovered a new leadership. On the day when the New York banks closed their doors, thus completing the " banking holiday ", Mr. Franklin Roosevelt became the President of the United States.

BOOK II

BATTLE

CHAPTER V

THE BATTLE BEGINS

UNTIL now the American resistance to Money, like the English resistance, had been instinctive, blind and leaderless. Upon the morning of Inauguration Day, March 4, 1933, resistance found a leader and became conscious. It gained direction and achieved the means of discipline—the essentials of victory.

"This great nation," declared the new President, "will endure as it has endured, will revive and will prosper." He went on to refer to "practices of the unscrupulous money-changers" which "stand indicted in the court of public opinion, rejected by the hearts and minds of men". And he concluded by saying that the people of the United States had "asked for discipline and direction under leadership".

The speech was a challenge to the Masters of Money. It was a re-statement of America's determination not to sacrifice her standard of living. Action followed. Mr. Roosevelt ordered the banks to remain closed and, virtually, took America off the Gold Standard. The pressure upon the American price-level of the high sterling price of gold was immediately relaxed. But the price of gold bounded up on the London bullion market to a new high record for all time. (Fig. 4.)

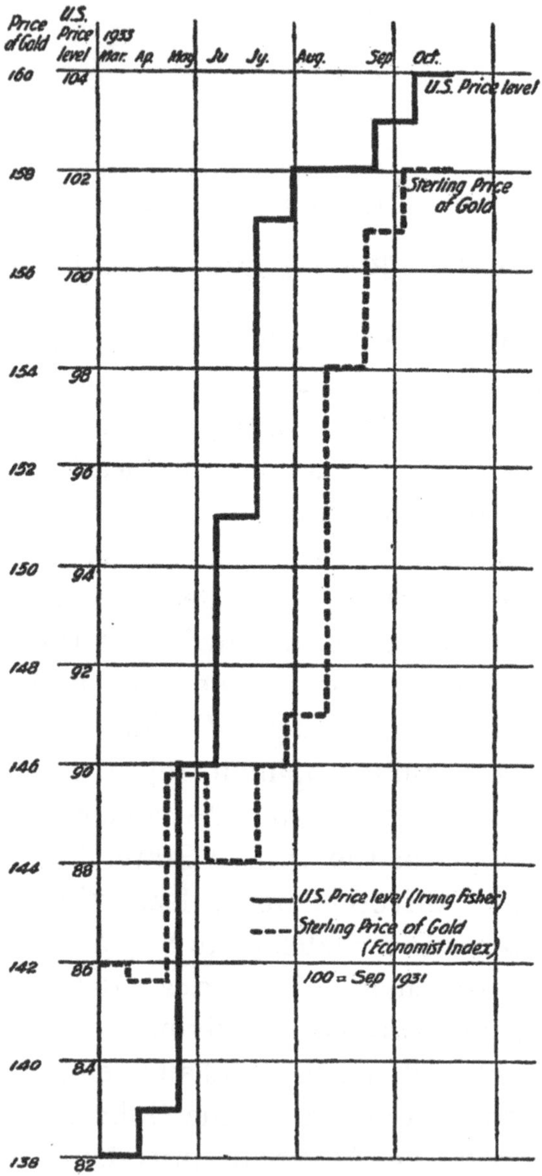

FIG. 4.—U.S. OFF GOLD.
Rise in sterling price of gold no longer depresses U.S. price-level.

The countries remaining upon gold—France, Italy, Germany, Switzerland, Holland and the rest—experienced an intensified pressure upon their prices. English prices, meanwhile, rose very little because the deflation of the continent of Europe threw large quantities of goods that could no longer be bought in France, Germany, and elsewhere, on to the English market. Mr. Roosevelt was receiving his first lesson in the power and resource of those whose private signatures are the money of the world.

Why did Europe not abandon the Gold Standard when America abandoned it? The way of escape from the pressure of the high sterling price of gold had been shown clearly and neither Frenchmen nor Germans were anxious to endure the distresses of a further fall in the level of prices. The answer is that Europe had experienced, only a few years earlier, the horrors of an inflation which, in the case of Germany, had wiped out all the people's savings, and in that of France had destroyed four-fifths of them. To these people the Gold Standard in any form was a haven of refuge in a tornado; arguments about stable money, where they were concerned, fell on deaf ears.

The Masters of Money possessed, therefore, in the European Gold *bloc* a means of preventing that rise in world prices which was the object of the President of the United States and the hope of all mankind. Each time the price of gold on the London market rose, the Gold *bloc* would be compelled further to cut its prices—that is to say, to reduce wages and other costs and so restrict buying-power. Restricted buying-power means restricted consumption of goods which means, again, surplus goods flung on to such markets as may be able to absorb them or left upon home markets to depress prices.

The effect of the rise in the sterling price of gold on the French price-level was disastrous. The same effect was being exerted, though in varying degrees, throughout the continent of Europe. President Roosevelt, therefore, if he was to succeed in restoring the prosperity of America and so of the world had to disarm the Masters of Money by taking from them their power to raise the sterling price of gold. There, in that power, resided the secret of their strength; for that power secured, by attracting gold from hoards and mines, a plentiful supply with which to pay for indispensable American goods and that power effectually prevented the rise of prices which must have depleted, more quickly, the existing gold resources. So long as Europe could pay in gold for American goods, so long was the danger that prices throughout the world must be stabilized likely to be averted. The demand of the Masters of Money was for gold and still more gold at such a sterling price that Europe would be forced to go on deflating, throwing goods on to the markets and depressing prices. The highest possible price for gold, the lowest possible prices for goods so that there might never, at any time, be a lack of gold to pay America. In addition, as little buying as possible from America.

It is necessary to call attention to the fact that this policy was bound to perpetuate the slump and thus to inflict grave hardship not upon America only but also upon the British Dominions. That the National Government in England exerted its utmost endeavours to bring the country and the Empire out of the slump there can be no doubt. But what could any English government do against a power which was able, certainly, to inflict starvation on these islands? Those who blame governments forget that "money has no motherland" and that it consists of the signatures of private persons. The world had tasted already of the wrath of a power about which even great statesmen, for example Disraeli, Mr. Gladstone and the late Lord Milner, have confessed their ignorance, while emphasizing their knowledge of its reality. There was no nation of Europe or of Asia which dared to defy that power or which, keeping in view the duty of governments to protect their peoples, could have dared. The world was in bondage to a monster which never yet had allowed any defiance to pass unpunished.

But the President of the United States stood in a special and peculiar position. America is the largest self-sufficient area in the world. There are thousands of miles of ocean to east and west while to north and south lie friendly and relatively small countries, Canada and Mexico. Armies cannot march against America; she cannot be attacked from the air; she can scarcely be attacked from the sea. Her food supply can never be in danger from a foreign enemy. She has nothing indeed to fear—as Mr. Roosevelt told her—but fear itself.

Again, thanks to the War, the tariff and the return of Europe to the Gold Standard, America, in 1933, was in possession of nearly one-half of the total gold stock of the world. Gold exports had been taking place on a great scale but the new President had stopped them. Mr. Roosevelt possessed the confidence of the whole people—the people who had defied the Masters of Money during thirteen years and who had remained unbroken by the collapse of 1929, the punishment inflicted by England's abandonment of the Gold Standard and the nation-wide banking crisis. That people was becoming aware of the causes of its misfortunes. It had neither respect for nor confidence in its financial and industrial leaders, and, consequently, was not likely to be stampeded by any interested propaganda. Here was the only general and the only army in the world capable of giving battle to the monster.

But if Mr. Roosevelt had no need to fear foreign invasion or open insurrection at home he had need to fear the effects, throughout the world, of a system which is essentially international and world-wide. The new President was not numbered among those persons who believed that America could isolate herself from the community of peoples. He understood very well that the war on which he was entering was a war for world recovery as well as for American recovery, and that if world recovery could not be accomplished America would eventually and inevitably succumb. That is obvious when it is recalled that the structure of American economic life was based, and had, for a century, been based, on an exchange of goods with Europe and Asia. American cotton, for example, was the raw material of Lancashire and the Far East. American tobacco supplied the needs of the English market and so on. America was not able, however rich she might be in buying-power, to absorb her production of these goods. In the case of cotton she did not possess the means to spin more than a fraction of the raw product, and retail buyers do not purchase bales of cotton. Consequently, if world trade was to be abandoned, a new foundation of economic life must be found. In that case it would be necessary to transfer to new uses the cotton fields of the Mississippi and to find new means of livelihood for a large negro population.

Mr. Roosevelt understood, however, that the Masters of Money would exert themselves to the utmost to reduce the exports of American cotton and other farm products, so as to reduce directly the flow of gold to America. It was necessary, therefore, in the first instance, to act as if America was isolated from the world and to reduce production as nearly as possible to the level of probable consumption.

This decision needed courage because farmers always and properly dislike methods of crop restriction. But it was necessary if the price pattern of the United States was to be corrected. The general level of prices had fallen, since 1926, by about 40 per cent. But of the components of this general level, farm prices had fallen 60 per cent whereas factory prices had fallen only 35 per cent. In other words the farmer's buying-power had shrunk to 40 per cent of its 1926 level, whereas the prices of the goods which the farmer bought had remained at 65 per cent of the 1926 level. The farmer was selling at 40 and buying at 65.

So faulty a price pattern is, of course, equivalent to national ruin in a country with a great farming population. Farmers' prices therefore had to be raised not only absolutely but also in relation to factory prices. The rate of rise of farmers' prices must, if the pattern was to be corrected, exceed considerably the rate of rise of factory prices. Mr. Roosevelt introduced two measures to secure these ends, the first called the Agricultural Adjustment Act (A.A.A.) and the second called the National Recovery Act (N.R.A.). Both Acts were designed to raise prices, but N.R.A. was designed, also, to prevent too steep a rise of industrial prices while farm prices, both by reason of the measures of crop restriction and by reason of a general increase in industrial wages, were rising. N.R.A. was launched with much propaganda, under the sign of a " blue eagle " which all those employers who agreed to abide by the Act displayed publicly. These Acts were not immediately successful because the price of gold in London continued to rise and so to cause deflation on the European continent and elsewhere. The American price-level was checked in its rise and the price pattern remained uncorrected.

Meanwhile, on May 7, 1933, Mr. Roosevelt made clear the aim of his monetary policy—namely, a stable price-level.

> The administration [he said] has the definite objective of raising commodity prices to such an extent that those who have borrowed money will, on the average, be able to repay that money in the same kind of dollar which they borrowed.
>
> We do not seek to let them get such a cheap dollar that they will be able to pay back a great deal less than they borrowed. In other words we seek to correct a wrong and not to create another wrong in the opposite direction.

This statement confirmed the worse fears of the Masters of Money. But there seems to have existed, nevertheless, some hope that the President's attitude would be changed by the World Economic Conference to which he was sending a delegation. In consequence a great deal of flattery was bestowed on Mr. Roosevelt in those organs of the European press which commonly reflect the views of moneylenders.

The World Economic Conference was opened in London on June 12, 1933; sixty-six nations took part in it. It owed its origin to the Lausanne Conference of the year before, at which the League of Nations had been asked "to convoke at a convenient date . . . a conference on Monetary and Economic Questions". Its effective life was exactly three weeks. At the end of that period President Roosevelt, from a warship on which he was taking a short holiday, addressed to it—in response to many pleas for a statement of his views—the following message:

> I would regard it as a catastrophe, amounting to a world tragedy, if the great conference of Nations called to bring about a more real and permanent financial

stability and a greater prosperity to the masses of all nations should in advance of any serious effort to consider these broader problems, allow itself to be diverted by the proposal of a purely artificial and temporary experiment affecting the monetary exchange of a few nations only.

Such action and such diversion show a singular lack of proportion and failure to remember the larger purposes for which the economic conference originally was called together.

I do not relish the thought that insistence on such action should be made the excuse for continuance of the basic economic errors that underlie so much of the present world-wide depression.

The world will not long be lulled by a specious fallacy of achieving a temporary and probably artificial stability in foreign exchange on the part of a few large countries only.

The sound, internal economic system of a nation is a greater factor in its well-being than the price of its currency in changing terms of the currencies of the nations.

It is for this reason that a reduced cost of government, adequate government income and ability to service its government debts are all so important to ultimate stability.

So, too, old fetishes of international bankers are being replaced by efforts to plan national currencies with the objective of giving to those currencies a *continuing purchasing-power which does not greatly vary in terms of commodities* and the need of modern civilization.

Let me be frank in saying that the United States seeks *the kind of dollar which, a generation hence, will have the same purchasing and debt-paying power as the dollar value we hope to attain in the near future.* That objective means more to the good of other nations than a fixed ratio for a month or two in terms of the pound or franc.

Our broad purpose is *permanent stabilization of every nation's currency.* Gold or gold and silver can well continue to be a metallic reserve behind currencies but this is not the time to dissipate gold reserves. When the world works out concerted policies in the majority of nations to produce balanced budgets and living within their means, then we can properly discuss a better distribution of the world's gold and silver supply to act as a reserve base for the National Currencies.

Restoration of world trade is an important factor both in the means and the result. Here, also, temporary exchange-fixing is not the true answer. We must rather mitigate existing embargoes to make easier the exchange of products which one nation has and another nation has not.

The conference was called to better—and perhaps to cure—fundamental economic ills. It must not be diverted from that effort.

These words were written by a man who had just rescued the price-level of his country from the depressing effect of the rising sterling price of gold (see Figs. 3 and 4). Mr. Roosevelt saw, of course, that, if a general return should be made to the foreign-loan Gold Standard, the conditions which had obtained before the collapse of 1929 must soon obtain again. He saw, also, and in consequence, that what was really being demanded was the removal of the American tariff without any pledges to stabilize European price-levels. Had he agreed to the conditions likely to be demanded he would have been partner to the restoration not of the automatic Gold Standard but of the foreign-loan Gold Standard of the Masters of Money, and Wall Street would instantly have become the world's chief moneylender. Agreement, without removal of the tariff, would, on the other hand, have restored to Lombard Street her ancient position as financial centre because, in that case, much of the "short-term money", i.e. the hoarded money, in New York banks would have been transferred by its owners to London. This would have caused, in the act of transfer, a big buying of pounds with dollars and hence a sharp fall of the dollar as against the pound. Mr. Roosevelt would, therefore, have been compelled to part with gold in order to keep himself upon the Gold Standard to which he had just returned. In either event—whether the American tariff was removed or whether it was not removed—the foreign-loan type of Gold Standard would soon have been in operation once more throughout the world.

It is important that the reader should form in his mind a clear picture of the relationship between the foreign exchange market and the Gold Standard, upon which relationship the hopes of the Masters of Money were set. As has already been pointed out the great bulk of the money of the world consists of the signatures of a few private persons. These signatures or I O Us purport to be promises to pay gold on demand, consequently, when a country is on the Gold Standard the holder of signature-money can walk into his bank and ask for gold. It follows that if a moment happens to arrive when something which the holder of signature-money wishes to buy can be obtained more cheaply by tendering gold than by tendering signature-money equivalent in face value to the gold, the signature-money will be cashed for gold. Such a moment arrives when one national currency, for example the pound sterling, is being bought in large amounts with another national currency, for example the dollar. Pounds, by reason of the demand for them, rise in value and go on rising until they become relatively very dear. At that point the holder of dollars recalls the fact that his dollars can be changed into gold at a fixed rate and that the gold so obtained can be changed into pounds, also at a fixed rate. Why then go on buying pounds with dollars at a higher price when pounds can be bought with the gold for which these same dollars can be exchanged?

In such circumstances dollars are cashed for gold in large quantities and the gold is then shipped out of America. As it goes it brings about, of course, a diminution of buying-power in America—that country being on the Gold Standard and consequently having its money linked to gold.

How clearly all this was seen by the President is obvious from his declaration: "this is not the time to dissipate gold reserves." Mr. Roosevelt, indeed, must have felt some surprise that it should have been thought possible to obtain his consent to the measures proposed. Was it likely, for example, that a nation which had tasted severe affliction in order to maintain its tariff and its standard of living would consent, now that better days were in sight, to abandon the position it had defended so stoutly? It was known that Mr. Roosevelt could not remove the tariff without the consent of Congress. Again, was it likely that a man who had just placed an embargo on the export of gold from his country was going to embrace a policy which must, immediately, result in a further export of gold? It would seem that the Masters of Money misread grossly the temper of the American resistance and, at the same time, under-estimated even more grossly the courage and instruction of the new President.

The Masters of Money appear, indeed, to have supposed that their blandishments must prove irresistible. They could promise, if their demands were fully conceded, to make an immediate end of the great depression in the manner in which an end of depression had been made by them in England after the Napoleonic wars when their demands—namely, repeal of the Corn Laws, removal of the English tariff, and a policy of Free Trade—had been conceded. Big foreign loans from New York and London would unquestionably have created a brisk export trade and prices would as unquestionably have bounded up—until the time was ripe for the inevitable slump by which under the Debt System the supply of borrowers is refreshed. Happily, the Dead Sea fruit was rejected and the Conference brought to an end, which must, in the circumstances, be looked upon as ignominious, seeing that the representatives of nearly all the nations in the world had nothing better to offer the world—with its 30,000,000 unemployed persons—than a return to the old system. Is it really to be believed that in all that array of experience and capacity there was none possessed of the same clear knowledge as Mr. Roosevelt? The frantic efforts to "save" the Conference, which were made when it became clear that the President of the United States was not to be won over will afford historians ample opportunity of comment upon human fatuity.

It should be noted, however, that the charge that Mr. Roosevelt deliberately, before the conference, misled the world about his views can be refuted out of his own mouth. Not for a day had he hidden his views from the world and on the eve of the Conference, on May 7th, after he had received the representatives of a large number of foreign nations he told the American people, in a wireless address:

> I want to emphasize to you that the domestic situation is inevitably and deeply tied in with the conditions in all of the other nations of the world. In other words we can get, in all probability, a fair measure of prosperity return in the United States, but it will not be permanent unless we get a return to prosperity all over the world.
>
> In the conferences which we have held and are holding with the leaders of other nations we are seeking four great objectives: First, a general reduction of armaments. . . . Second, a cutting down of trade barriers, in order to restart the flow of *exchange* of crops and goods among nations. Third, the setting up of a stabilization of currencies in order that trade can make contracts ahead. Fourth, the re-establishment of friendly relations and greater confidence among all nations.

There was no refusal in this statement either to adjust tariffs or to stabilize currencies; there was refusal to adjust tariffs except for the purpose of an exchange of crops and goods ("Yankee Trading") and to stabilize currencies before such exchange had been secured. If the statesmen who visited the President did not know the difference between the automatic Gold Standard, as described in every text-book of economics and the foreign-loan Gold Standard of the Masters of Money as used during the whole course of the Nineteenth Century, that fault of ignorance cannot be blamed upon Mr. Roosevelt. Indeed, it is clear that Mr. Roosevelt thought that the statesmen who visited him shared his views, because, in the same wireless address he declared:

> Our foreign visitors, these past three weeks, have responded to these purposes in a very helpful way. All of the nations have suffered alike in this great depression. They have all reached the conclusion that each can best be helped by the common action of all. It is in this spirit that our visitors have met with us and discussed our common problems. The international conference that lies before us must succeed. The future of the world demands it and we have each of us pledged ourselves to the best joint efforts to this end."

The American delegation to the World Economic Conference had, however, one suggestion to offer in which Mr. Roosevelt was deeply interested—namely the raising of the price of silver. America announced her readiness to buy silver with the object of raising the price and the sixty-six nations represented at the Conference pledged themselves to help. The "London Silver Agreement" was signed. The Masters of Money, on this occasion, expressed themselves as well pleased. They saw that, if America was prepared to take payment for goods in silver as well as in gold, their anxieties about the supply of gold to pay for American goods would be lightened.

What they did not see was that silver was destined to play a chief part in Mr. Roosevelt's plan of campaign. Twice over, during this London Conference, indeed, these Masters of Money under-estimated their opponent and so fell into errors destined, in the event, to prove fatal to their hopes. By demanding the stabilization of currencies, they showed their hand at a moment when they ought to have gone to almost any length to avoid such exposure. By blessing the Silver Agreement they helped to fashion the weapon that was destined to destroy them.

The World Economic Conference had no sooner broken up than a sharp rise in the sterling price of gold began—that shown in Fig. 4. The French price-level immediately underwent a heavy fall and the rise in the farm prices in America slowed down owing to the restriction of Continental buying of cotton and other materials. An inspired propaganda, to the effect that no recovery could possibly take place until the demands of the Masters of Money had been conceded, continued throughout this period not only in America but in every country of the world. Support was lent to it by the fact that the heavy buying of gold on the London market was making the pound a "weak" currency and thus, relatively, forcing up the value of the dollar. Towards the end of the summer of 1933 the dollar was actually becoming so much "over-valued" in relation to the pound that it was difficult to sell American goods in the sterling area. Thus, to the pressure of the Continental deflation was added the pressure of the rising dollar. Mr. Roosevelt tried to ease this latter burden by selling dollars but the policy did not succeed. On October 22, 1933, therefore he told the nation:

> Some people are putting the cart before the horse. They want a permanent revaluation of the dollar first. It is the Governments' policy to restore the price-level first. . . .
>
> When we have restored the price-level we shall seek to establish and maintain a dollar which will not change its purchasing and debt paying power during the succeeding generation. I said that in my message to the American delegation in London last July. And I say it now, once more.
>
> Because of conditions in this country and because of events beyond our control in other parts of the world, it becomes increasingly important to develop and apply the further measures which may be necessary from time to time to control the gold value of our own dollar at home.
>
> Our dollar is now altogether too greatly influenced by the accidents of international trade, by the internal policies of other nations and by political disturbance in other continents. Therefore the United States must take firmly in its own hands the control of the gold value of our dollar. This is necessary in order to prevent dollar disturbances from swinging us away from our ultimate goal, namely the continued recovery of our commodity prices.

The President then announced that he would buy gold newly mined in the United States at prices to be determined from time to time. In effect he was setting up a market for gold in New York in opposition to the market for gold in London.

CHAPTER VI

TACTICS

PRESIDENT ROOSEVELT'S "Gold-buying policy", as it was called, was received in financial circles with the kind of tolerance which a guest displays towards his host's ill-behaved child. Money affected to be amused as well as a little surprised.

Actually the new policy occasioned the greatest uneasiness. For it was obviously a first step of the return journey to some kind of Gold Standard, and none of the Masters of Money was so sanguine as to suppose that it was the foreign-loan Gold Standard to which Mr. Roosevelt was marching. But if he was going back to the automatic Gold Standard then he must be holding, up his sleeve, some device by which to prevent that standard being turned, once again, to the uses of moneylenders.

So great was the anxiety to discover what this device might be that bankers all over the world began to urge the President to return immediately to the Gold Standard, *as the only solid foundation for international lending*. These attempts to draw the badger evoked no response from the White House; but on the last day of the year 1933 the President issued a statement "On Purchase and Coinage of Silver", which sent a chill of dismay through every bank parlour in the world. In this statement a careful summary was made of the agreement about silver entered into by the sixty-six governments at the World Economic Conference in London. Mr. Roosevelt said:

> It will be remembered that, at the London Conference, sixty-six governments unanimously adopted the silver resolution proposed by our Government, providing in substance that these Governments:
>
> Would refrain from the policy and practice of melting up and debasing silver coins:
>
> Would replace low valued paper money with silver coins:
>
> Would not enact legislation that would depreciate the value of silver in the world market. . . .
>
> India had the power to dispose of, on the markets of the world, at any time and at any price hundreds of millions of ounces of silver. In fact India had the power and capacity to dump silver derived from the melting up of Indian silver coins in an amount equal to the world's production from the mines for the period of two years. This power and the uncertainty attending its execution was destructive of the value and stability of silver throughout the world.
>
> China agreed, during the period of four years, commencing January 1st, 1934 and ending January 1st, 1938 not to permit the sale of any silver derived from the debasing or melting up of silver coins.
>
> India agreed to limit the sales of such silver to a maximum of 35,000,000 ounces, annually, during such period, and
>
> Spain agreed not to sell in excess of 5,000,000 ounces of such silver annually during such period.
>
> After such sales, these Governments are to be bound by the general resolution adopted at the London Conference.
>
> As a condition of the agreement by China, India and Spain, however, it was required that Australia, Canada,

> Mexico, Peru and the United States should take silver from the production of their respective mines to the gross amount of 35,000,000 ounces annually for such period of four years. The United States by reason of its large population and its large silver production, agreed to take from its mines annually at least 24,421,410 ounces of silver during such period. The production of the United States for 1932 was, approximately 24,000,000 ounces.

The London Silver Agreement, as this summary makes clear, amounted to a damming-up of potential supplies of silver while efforts were being made to raise the price of the metal. India had put the agreement into effect before December 1933. Mr. Roosevelt now affirmed his readiness to buy the quota of silver assigned to him and announced, further, that he was prepared to mint into coins all silver mined in the United States, at the rate of 64½ cents an ounce.

Since the existing silver coinage of the United States contained such quantities of the metal as to make silver worth $1.29 cents an ounce in terms of that coinage, the President was about to charge a fee for minting (a so-called " seignorage " fee) of 50 per cent of the value of the silver.

Stiff, however, as that seignorage or minting fee was, the price offered for the silver was far higher than the existing world price. From having been a precious metal silver had sunk to a value little higher than that of tobacco. It had lost some four-fifths of its value and thus the silver-using peoples, (more than one-third of mankind) had lost four-fifths of their buying-power. This fall had occurred when the fall in world prices occurred—from 1929 onwards as is clearly shown in Fig. 1.

Mr. Roosevelt, by re-opening his mint to silver, was taking the first step towards making that metal a money once more. He was, therefore, in some sort, setting up a silver as well as a Gold Standard. The moment his proclamation was published the Masters of Money knew by what means it was proposed to secure the effective working of the automatic Gold Standard.

Their anxiety will be understood if the relationship or ratio between the price of silver and the price of gold is held in mind. If for example gold costs $35 an ounce in America and silver costs $1, then the ratio is 35 : 1. In other words, the Chinaman or Indian wishing to buy an ounce of gold in America, in order to make purchases in that country, will have to expend 35 ounces of silver. Suppose, however, that the English price of gold is 140*s.* an ounce and the English price of silver is 5*s.* an ounce, then the English ratio will be 28 : 1. The Chinaman or Indian will be able in that event to buy an ounce of gold in London for a smaller quantity of silver than would be required to buy an ounce of gold in New York. In such circumstances the East will buy in London, and New York will lose the Eastern trade unless she makes a change in her silver–gold ratio.[1]

If two countries are on the Gold Standard and, in

[1] For the same reason the East would sell in New York. Thus, the money obtained in New York would be spent in London. Gold would tend to flow from New York to London.

consequence, have fixed prices for gold, the silver–gold ratio can be changed, in either case, only by buying or selling silver, that is to say by raising or lowering the price of silver. But if for example one country is offering a higher price for silver than the other, the merchants of the low-price country will sell silver to the high-price country and so bring the price down again, always provided that the Government of the high-price country does not go on buying, at the high price, all the silver offered to it. If the Government of the high-price country does go on buying in that fashion then, as the world stocks of silver become exhausted, the price of the metal in the low-price country will rise. And, meanwhile, the high-price country will have been showing a different gold–silver ratio from the low-price country. If the low-price country happens to have a big Oriental trade, the loss of that trade, occasioned by the adverse ratio, will, in all probability, force its Government to hasten the rise of the silver price.

It is obvious that, if such a price-raising policy is to succeed, the Government embarking upon the policy must be ready to buy very large quantities of silver and, further, that it must possess some assurance that huge, undisclosed hoards will not, suddenly, be flung upon its markets. The London Silver Agreement gave Mr. Roosevelt that assurance. The eagerness of America to return to a bi-metallic standard guaranteed an almost insatiable demand for the metal.

The Masters of Money saw, therefore, suddenly, the possibility that international price-levels might be stabilized and held stable by means of the agreement which they themselves had blessed only a few months earlier. For if a country was trying to keep a lower price-level than the United States, and so drawing buyers and their gold from America, Mr. Roosevelt would buy silver to replace the departing gold and thus raise the price of silver. The country with the lower price-level would now be compelled to buy silver also or lose its Eastern trade. Buying silver puts money out (to buy the silver with) into markets and so raises the buyer's price-level. Here then was the old automatic Gold Standard fitted with a new safety device in the shape of a silver pendulum. Here perhaps was stabilization of the price-levels of all nations and therefore a world-wide march out of debt.

But lively as were the fears engendered by the Silver Policy, they were not fears for the immediate future. True, India and China were pledged by the London Agreement not to melt down their currencies and dump great hoards of silver on the world's markets. But the quantities of silver available were so enormous that it seemed impossible that Mr. Roosevelt's price of 64½ cents would easily be reached. That price is equivalent (at $5 to £1) to about *2s. 8¼d.* an ounce and the price of silver in London was about *1s. 8d.* an ounce. The London price of silver did not in fact rise to any important extent and, after the usual crop of contemptuous references to "monetary manipulators" had filled the newspapers of the world for a few days, the white metal was, apparently, forgotten.

Attention, on the contrary, was focused upon its

yellow rival. Mr. Roosevelt's policy of buying newly-mined American gold had not effected any notable change in the value of the dollar, which remained high in relation to the pound. It became clear, therefore, that if change was to be effected purchases of gold must be made outside of as well as inside of America—the United States, in short, must go back to the Gold Standard. Mr. Roosevelt was in a difficulty. He had, as has been seen, refused to go back to the Gold Standard at the World Economic Conference because he had realized that such return was likely to be followed by a heavy outflow of the metal from New York. How could he go back now without incurring such an outflow? His gold policy of January 15th, 1934 (which thus followed the first announcement of his silver policy by only a fortnight) was his answer to that question. The gold policy was announced to Congress in the following speech, every word of which deserves the reader's close attention.

> In conformity with the progress we are making in restoring a fairer price-level and with our purpose of arriving eventually at a less variable purchasing-power for the dollar, I ask the Congress for certain additional legislation to improve our financial and monetary system. By making clear that we are establishing permanent metallic reserves in the possession and ownership of the Federal Government, we can organize a currency system that will be both sound and adequate.
>
> The issuance and control of the means of exchange which we call " money " is a high prerogative of government. It has been such for many centuries. Because they were scarce, because they could readily be subdivided and transported, gold and silver have been used

either for money or as a basis for forms of money which, in themselves, had only nominal intrinsic value.

In pure theory, of course, a government could issue mere tokens to serve as money—tokens which would be accepted at their face value if it were certain that the amount of these tokens was permanently limited and confined to the total amount necessary for the daily cash needs of the community. Because this assurance could not always or sufficiently be given governments have found that reserves or bases of gold and silver behind their paper or token currency added stability to their financial systems.

There is still much confusion of thought which prevents a world-wide agreement creating a uniform monetary policy. Many advocate gold as the sole basis of currency; others advocate silver; still others advocate both gold and silver, whether as separate bases or on a basis with a fixed ratio or on a fixed basis. We hope that, despite present world confusion, events are leading to some future form of general agreement. The recent London Agreement in regard to silver was a step, though only a step, in this direction.

At this time we can usefully take a further step, which, we hope, will contribute to an ultimate world-wide solution. . . .

It is a prudent step to vest in the government of a nation the title to and possession of all monetary gold within its boundaries and to keep that gold in the form of bullion rather than in coin. Because the safe keeping of this monetary basis rests with the Government, we have already called in the gold which was in the possession of private individuals or corporations. There remains, however, a very large weight in gold bullion and coins which is still in the possession or control of the Federal Reserve Banks.

Although, under existing law, there is authority, by executive act, to take title to the gold in the possession or control of the Reserve Banks, this is a step of such importance that I prefer to ask the Congress by specific enactment to vest in the United States Government, title to all supplies of American-owned monetary gold with provision for the payment therefor in gold certificates. . . .

Such legislation places the right, title and ownership to our gold reserves in the Government itself; it makes clear the Government's ownership of any added dollar-value of the country's stock of gold which would result from any decrease of the gold content of the dollar which may be made in the public interest. It would also of course, with equal justice, cast upon the Government the loss of such dollar value if the public interest in the future should require an increase in the amount of gold designated as a dollar.

The title to all gold being in the Government, the total stock will serve as a permanent and fixed metallic reserve which will change in amount only so far as necessary for the settlement of international balances or as may be required by a future agreement among the nations of the world for a redistribution of the world stock of monetary gold.

Mr. Roosevelt added in reference to silver:

Governments can well, as they have in the past, employ silver as a basis for currency and I look for a greatly increased use.

The revaluation of the dollar was then discussed. Mr. Roosevelt pointed out that he had power already to devalue it 50 per cent. He asked Congress to fix the upper limit to which devaluation might be carried out at 60 per cent—thus giving him power to reduce the gold-value of the dollar by from 40 to 50 per cent or, in other terms, to buy gold at prices 40 to 50 per cent higher than the old, fixed rate of $20 to the ounce.

The Gold Standard had been restored. But it was a movable and not a fixed standard seeing that Mr.

Roosevelt might, at will, change the gold value of the dollar between fixed limits. Again it was a standard whereby the dollar was made cheaper than the currencies still on the gold *bloc* so that the price of gold in New York was higher than the price of gold in Paris. Gold would therefore flow from Paris to New York until the two prices were brought into line. Gold would not flow out of New York to Paris because of the ever-present danger that France might come off the Gold Standard.

These are technical matters of less importance than the great central fact that the basis of money in America was no longer the signatures of private persons but the signature of the head of the State. The new Gold Certificates were Mr. Roosevelt's promises to pay gold which he actually held under his hand and which none but he, as President, might hold. What therefore the private lenders of credit in America would in future be lending across their banking counters would be, not their promises to pay gold but their promises to pay notes based on the President's promises to pay gold. And since silver had been added to gold as a basis of the President's promises, it was clear that such losses of gold to foreign countries as might be incurred could always be made good by buying silver. In other words the quantity of money in the markets of America was no longer to be subject to any movements of gold. Mr. Roosevelt had taken the American price-level out of the control of the Masters of Money. He had, in addition, turned their device of signature-money against themselves.

But what he had not yet done was to make it impossible for them to buy up the price of gold on the London market and so prevent world prices from rising. The accomplishment of that supreme object of his policy depended, first and foremost, on his silver policy and, after that, on his policy to restore the price pattern within America. If the silver policy succeeded, the price of gold in London would necessarily be the same as the price of gold in New York, because any difference would be reflected at once in the ratio between gold and silver, that is to say in the volume of the Eastern trade. The crucial question, therefore, was whether or not Mr. Roosevelt could maintain his price for silver and force London to adopt it. If he could do that, the London price of gold must be the same as his price, and consequently the English and the world price-levels must approximate closely to his price-level. The slump would be over. The automatic Gold Standard, with its silver pendulum, would be in action. Mankind would be delivered. Battle was joined, at the beginning of 1934, on this issue.

CHAPTER VII

SIEGE

It is not to be supposed that in February 1934 the Masters of Money despaired in any way of the issue of battle. How many battles had not they and their predecessors fought and won against earlier stabilizers of the level of prices—Napoleon, for example? If Mr. Roosevelt's silver policy was potentially dangerous, at least it had relieved the strain on gold—as they had foreseen. With the United States pledged to take payment for goods in both metals, the day was distant when it would be necessary to pay for goods with goods—in other words to agree to stabilize prices.

Nevertheless, there was great anxiety to know if the gold *bloc*, or any member of it, would try to follow Mr. Roosevelt in effecting a devaluation of currency. The monetary objections to devaluation have already been mentioned; in addition, political objections of a serious kind obtained. The most important of these was, of course, the anxiety felt in France about German re-armament. That the Masters of Money had helped to re-arm Germany has been asserted again and again, but evidence is unobtainable. It cannot be disputed, on the other hand, that the spectacle of a Germany becoming stronger and more aggressive daily was a substantial reason, in French minds, for refusing to make any change in monetary policy. Even in Italian minds the spectacle was not without its appeal, and what France and Italy thought the smaller countries associated with them thought also. Further, any hankerings which French politicians may have felt towards devaluation must have been dismissed after the so-called Stavisky riots in Paris which, by a coincidence, had occurred simultaneously with President Roosevelt's devaluation proposals and which had led to the fall of the Government of M. Chautemps and to the establishing of a National Union Government under the aged M. Doumergue.

" Devaluation of the franc," M. Doumergue declared, " must result in civil war at home and then in foreign invasion."

The Governor of the Bank of France, M. Moret, concurred in these views and, consequently, as the sterling price of gold, which had fallen somewhat during the late autumn, bounded up again to a new high record for all time (140*s.* an ounce) the French price-level began to fall once more. But steep as was this fall—and it was very steep—it was as nothing to the fall in the level of Chinese prices which began in January 1934, immediately after the announcement, on December 31, 1933, of the new buying-price for silver.

This fall in Chinese prices, as a glance at Fig. 5 will show, was not due to any marked rise in the price of silver, which remained more or less stationary around 1*s.* 8*d.* an ounce. It must, therefore, have been due to loss of silver through smuggling in order to sell the

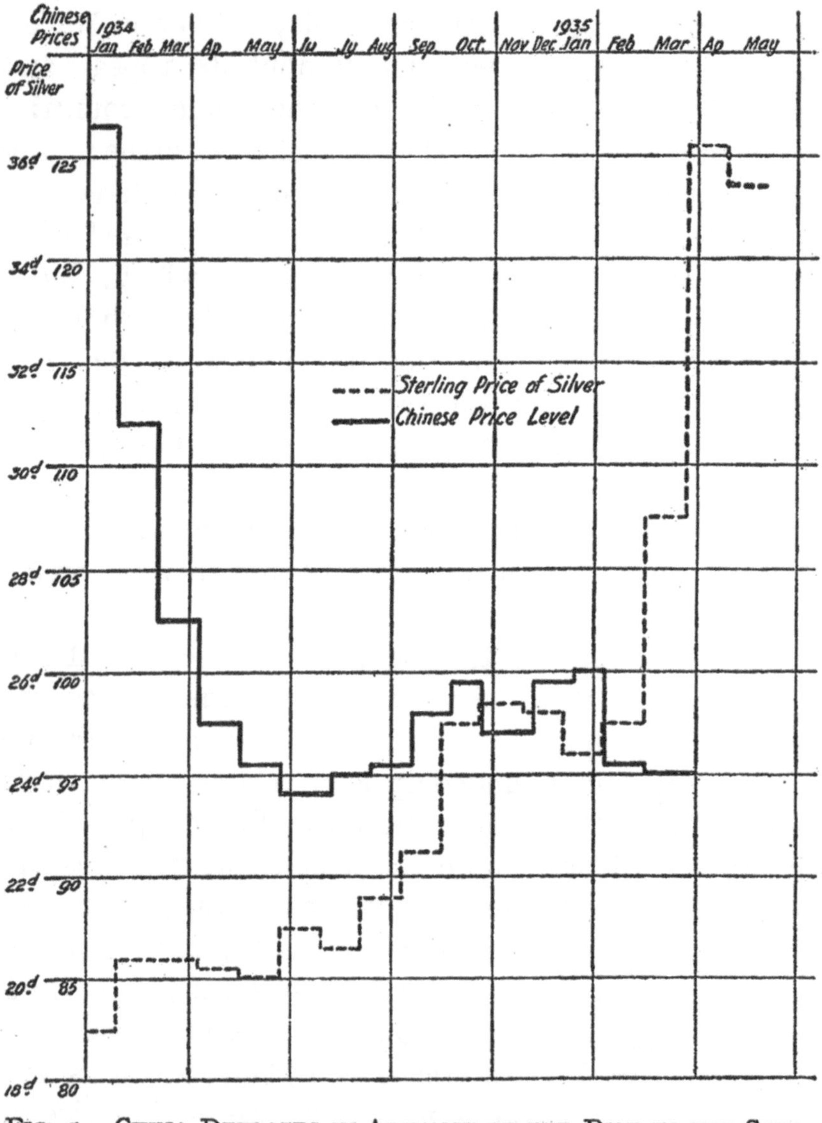

FIG. 5.—CHINA DEFLATES IN ADVANCE OF THE RISE IN THE STERLING PRICE OF SILVER.

metal to America at the higher American price. The Chinese Government was pledged, as has been seen, by the London agreement; the Government did everything in its power to stop the smuggling without, however, achieving much success. In consequence the sterling price of silver remained much below Mr. Roosevelt's price (2*s.* 8*d.*).

The Chinese smuggling was welcome, undoubtedly, to the Masters of Money because it afforded a source of silver at a moment when, by reason of the London agreement, the chief sources were drying up. But the smuggling was, naturally, much less agreeable to Mr. Roosevelt who was trying to raise the silver price and so to increase the buying-power of the East. Because of the smuggling the trouble which it had been sought to guard against by the London agreement was in full operation—namely, a great outpouring of silver and a consequent deflation of the Chinese currency—the Shanghai silver dollar, based upon that metal.

There was thus active deflation both in West and East. In the West the cause was the rising sterling price of gold; in the East the smuggling of silver from China. West and East were losing their buying-power simultaneously. The task of raising American and world price-levels in such circumstances was a difficult one.

Mr. Roosevelt's chief concern, as has been said, was his farmers' price-level, and he was specially concerned about the price of wheat and the price of cotton. There have been enormous surplus stocks of these commodities in North America and elsewhere during the past few years. The wheat surpluses have been concentrated in Canada and Australia because the Argentine wheat, the only other large exportable surplus, has been used up, more or less completely, each year, for the most part in England. (Argentine wheat has been selling at 9*s.* per quarter less than Canadian wheat and at about 4*s.* per quarter less than Australian wheat. The preference granted to Dominion products at the Ottawa Conference was only, for wheat, 2*s.* per quarter.)

These surpluses afford some indication of the loss of buying-power sustained by the world. They prove that, whereas production has declined, consumption has declined even more rapidly and that, consequently, decline of consumption and not increase of production, caused the World Slump. Thus, they justify both Mr. Roosevelt's determination to restrict his crops and his attempt to increase consumption throughout the world.

But these surpluses do not tell the whole story of the ruin of wheat and cotton farmers in America and the British Empire. Monetary factors were also in play. Thus, though in 1934 Argentina surpassed both Canada and Australia in the matter of quantity of wheat exported to Great Britain, nevertheless, the value of the Argentine imports was considerably less than that of the Canadian imports. The Argentine peso was linked with sterling in such a fashion as to allow it to rise and fall with the price of wheat. As the price of wheat fell the Argentine farmer got more pesos for the pound and thus was able, easily, to undersell the Canadian and Australian farmer. Traders naturally buy in the cheapest market. The Argentine device of the movable peso came as it happened at a fortunate moment for the Masters of Money because Argentina owes much money to England and buys large amounts of English goods. It was possible to pay her, therefore, in goods and so to husband supplies of gold and silver for more urgent disbursement.

But the wheat picture as it presented early in 1934 would not be complete without mention of the dumping of flour upon the English market by Continental nations whose domestic buying-power was being destroyed by the deflation consequent on the re-valuation of the dollar and on the rising pound price of gold. Messrs. Spillers, the well-known firm of flour millers, pointed out at their annual meeting (*Times*, 6 June, 1935) that:

Imports (of flour) from France, Italy and Germany combined totalled:

1925	49,580	sacks of 280 lb.
1933	821,441	,, ,, ,,
1934	1,056,387	,, ,, ,,

The 1934 figures are more than 20 times the 1925 figures. The separate figures were:

France:		
1925	25,448	sacks of 280 lb.
1934	491,924	,, ,, ,,
Italy:		
1925	2,556	,, ,, ,,
1934	160,230	,, ,, ,,
Germany:		
1925	21,576	,, ,, ,,
1934	404,233	,, ,, ,,

Messrs. Spillers added:

> All this foreign flour is sold at very considerably below the cost of production as well as below the price charged in the country of origin. French milled flour has been sold here at 9*s.* 6*d.* per sack while the price in France at the current rate of exchange has not been lower than 56*s.* 0*d.*; Italian flour has been offered at as low a figure as 7*s.* 3*d.* per sack while the price in Italy is about 55*s.* 0*d.* German flour has been sold at 10*s.* 6*d.* per sack while the price in Germany has been in the neighbourhood of 61*s.* 0*d.* . . . Nearly 4,000,000 sacks of flour from all sources were imported in 1934.[1]

All this flour, of course, competed with wheat. In addition, competition came from the French Government which, late in 1934, dumped enormous quantities of wheat on the Liverpool and London markets at some 18*s.* a quarter, the price of Canadian wheat being about 30*s.* a quarter, of Australian about 24*s.*, and of Argentine about 20*s.* The Canadian, Australian and American wheat farmers, therefore, had to face, when attempting to enter the English markets:

1. The sliding peso of the Argentine farmer, with his lower costs of labour.
2. The dumped French wheat.
3. The dumped French, Italian and German flour.

And all this at a moment when the markets of West and East were shrinking, as has been seen, under the most terrible deflationary drives in history.

[1] These figures show also to what extremity France, Italy and Germany were driven in order to obtain sterling credits with which to buy colonial products, e.g. tea, rubber, etc. Sir Samuel Hoare touched on this subject in his speech to the League of Nations in September 1935.

The case of the American cotton farmer was, if anything, worse. Indian, Brazilian and Peruvian cottons are cheaper than American cotton. The decision of Brazil to grow larger quantities of cotton, which was taken in 1933, must be accounted another fortunate coincidence so far as the Masters of Money are concerned, because Brazil is a considerable buyer of British goods and has been, in the past, a substantial borrower.

It was with these difficulties, as well as with the (equally great) difficulties of his sugar growers, his tobacco growers, and the whole body of his meat farming industry that Mr. Roosevelt had to contend during the early months of 1934 when, as has been said, West and East—the whole round world—were in the grip of a new and even more savage deflation. He made heavy going and, instead of rising, his farmers' price-level sagged and fell away.

This fall, which especially affected wheat and cotton, was duly trumpeted abroad in all the organs of Money as proof that " no nation can live to itself " and that, consequently, every nation must attend its Master's voice. The itch for discourse and edification which has always characterized moneylenders in every age and which is never so lively as when their plans are succeeding, adds to the gaiety of life in times otherwise charged with distress and must therefore be accounted to them for righteousness. One has the heartening impression, as one reads these discourses, of Olympian heights from which the feeble and futile struggles of men are watched with an excellent detachment. And why not ? Is not the moneylender able to make trees blossom and flocks and herds multiply merely by writing his name upon little pieces of paper ? Cannot he fertilize deserts with the ink of his pen and, from his seat, send forth upon his fellows the early and the latter rain ? So it seemed, at any rate, to the whole world until, suddenly, out of a higher heaven than that in which moneylenders dwell, there came forth, early in the month of May 1934, great winds and a parching heat. The top spit of the American soil over millions of acres was lifted up, bodily, into the skies and, like a pall, drifted across plains and cities as a witness against this generation. The surpluses of wheat and cotton that were the hope of the Masters of Money were destroyed in large measure before their eyes.

In days to come men will speak of the Great Drought as of a great deliverance. For it changed the face of the world. From early in May 1934 the prices of wheat and cotton began to rise, while factory prices, thanks to N.R.A., remained more or less stationary. The American price pattern was at last in process of correction. This is shown in Fig. 8, page 107.

CHAPTER VIII

ASSAULT

THE Great Drought of 1934 removed those artificially created surpluses of wheat and cotton upon which the Masters of Money had counted to destroy the American President and all his works. Action, therefore, became necessary at once either to create new surpluses or to devise new weapons of offence. The currency drive which began as soon as the serious character of the drought was recognized was Money's reply to the drought.

The violence and scope of this assault deserve the most careful consideration and examination because they reveal the protean nature of the power of Money and display its ubiquitous character. Money was about to operate anti-nationally in the United States, in England, in France, in Belgium and in China, to mention only a few of its victims; but its action would be so carefully hidden that honest and patriotic men would serve its purposes and even its avowed enemies become, unwittingly, its tools.

The case of the United States is an example in point. In that country there were large groups of people who believed that, since the World Slump had been caused by deflation it could be cured by the opposite process

—namely, inflation. These groups demanded the issue and distribution of large sums of money created *de novo* by the Government. They expressed, and felt, astonishment that Mr. Roosevelt could not see eye to eye with them and, in their disappointment, became easy victims of those who whispered that the President was "in the hands of Wall Street", and that he was engaged in the futile enterprise of "trying to borrow himself out of debt".

These good people, in truth, had no knowledge of the real circumstances of the case. They did not realize that a war was in process with the strongest power which this world has known, or that all the Governments of the world, in presence of the Money Power, were sparrows in presence of a hawk. Had their ideas been carried out the inflation at which they aimed must inevitably have become, first a boom and then a catastrophe in which the value of the dollar would have disappeared. Consequently, Mr. Roosevelt had no choice but to act with all his strength against both the Veterans Bonus Lobby and the Silver Lobby, although both these organizations included sincere friends of his own. He was on holiday, fishing, when the inflationist agitation began. On his return he spoke, grimly, about having learned to catch sharks, calling himself, at the same time a "tough guy". Then he published, for the information of the simple, a list of the banks and other institutions which were large holders of silver. This list was produced in two parts, on two consecutive days. The first part gave the names beginning with the letters from A to H, the second with the letters from I to Z.

The effect of this rebuke was to impose silence on the two lobbies. The President lost no time in arming himself with powers by which future attacks might be resisted. On May 22nd, 1934, he sent a message to Congress informing that body that a bill would be introduced at once to increase the amount of silver in the monetary stocks of the country. The final object of this increase, he declared, was to maintain one-quarter *of the value* of the monetary stocks in silver and three-quarters of that value in gold. (If, for example, the monetary stocks amounted to $1, then silver to the value of 25 cents would be held along with gold to the value of 75 cents.)

The bill authorized and directed the Government to buy silver and gave the right to take possession of all domestic stocks at a price not exceeding 50·01 cents an ounce. The Government was empowered, further, " to regulate imports, exports and other dealings in monetary silver ". Mr. Roosevelt expressed the view that his proposals could be carried out " without seriously disturbing adjustments in world trade ", adding:

> Concerted action by all nations, or at least a large group of nations, is necessary if a permanent measure of value, including both gold and silver (i.e. the gold standard with the silver pendulum) is eventually to be made a world standard.

He declared that he had " begun to confer with some of our neighbours in regard to the use of both gold and silver ".

These neighbours were Canada and Mexico, both of

whom had suffered greatly by reason of the World Slump.

This silver bill was hailed by the uninstructed as a measure designed to raise to new heights the price of the white metal. In fact its object was to prevent sudden rises in that price and to defeat attempts to produce these rises. This becomes obvious when the position of China is considered. China, as has been seen, had been deprived by the Masters of Money first of her ancient Government and dynasty, then of her cohesion and finally of some four-fifths of her buying-power. It is doubtful, indeed, if history holds any more melancholy story than the dismemberment of this great Empire and the spiritual and moral degradation of this great people. The Manchu dynasty had ruled China with wisdom and restraint; at the moment of its fall at the hands of the bullies of international finance it had come near to ridding the people of the curse of opium. All that had been changed as soon as the ancient structure was destroyed. With the moneylender in possession China was divided up and given once more to the salesmen of debt and opium. Mr. Roosevelt's policy had coincided, in point of time, with the beginning of reaction against these horrors. In China, as in Japan, honest men, drawn for the most part from the soldier type, were beginning to offer an effective resistance. Chiang kai-Shek, the Chinese Generalissimo, is a conspicuous case in point.

Chiang kai-Shek, in 1934, had become in some sort the overlord of the three governments of China: the Pekin Government in the North, the Nanking Government in the Centre, and the Canton Government in the South. But these governments were by no means united and elements in them offered, from time to time, opposition to the leaders' plan to effect, once more, the union of China. A vast confusion obtained; in these troubled waters the Masters of Money were accustomed to fish with impunity.

The Nanking Government was the titular administration of China. Its money, the Shanghai silver dollar, was the Chinese currency. Consequently the smuggling operations which had begun as soon as Mr. Roosevelt's policy was announced, had placed this government in a difficult position. Silver was leaving Nanking and Shanghai in large amounts both by legitimate and illegitimate channels in order that advantage might be taken of the relatively high price of the metal obtaining outside of China. In these circumstances no further sharp rise in silver was to be desired; nor did Mr. Roosevelt's policy require any sharp rise. As has been pointed out, that policy was designed to provide a pendulum to the Gold Standard so that automatic working might be secured. Silver had to rise to some extent to make the pendulum effective but a fall in the sterling price of gold would have been equally effective. The President of the United States, indeed, was concerned to give buying-power to the Chinese market and not merely to juggle with precious metals. A moderate rise in silver was a means to that end and nothing more.

Consequently, Mr. Roosevelt was determined, as has been said, to prevent, so far as lay in his power, any attempt to force the price of silver to the uncomfortable heights to which, in London, the price of gold had been forced. The last thing that he aimed at achieving was the addition to the embarrassment of a boom in gold of the embarrassment of a boom in silver. The Masters of Money, on the contrary, saw in the American silver policy a means not only of defeating their opponent, but also of regaining over China the full control which General Chiang kai-Shek and his supporters were weakening. China as has been seen and as is shown in Fig. 5 had already, by April 1934, been deflated to the limit of the possible by means of exports of silver. If silver continued to leave the country the Nanking Government would be compelled, in order to save the native banks, to devalue the Shanghai dollar or, alternatively, to abandon the Silver Standard for the Gold Standard or the Sterling Standard. There were grave objections to devaluation, the chief of which was the fact that most of the silver coins in China are held in private possession and would, therefore, have been sold as silver if their face value had shrunk below their silver value. The issue, if silver was to be abandoned, lay, therefore, between the Gold Standard and the Sterling Standard, between that is to say the dollar, which was now back on gold, and the pound.

The Masters of Money desired that the money of China should be linked to the pound. If that could be accomplished the silver pendulum would be destroyed for ever because the price of silver would not then matter in the least to the Chinese importer. Silver would have become merely a form of sterling-money with a fixed relationship to sterling. The Masters of Money, therefore, were not anxious to stop smuggling but were, on the contrary, anxious to promote it by effecting a further sharp rise in the price of silver. They foresaw that such a rise must, quickly, produce a financial crisis in Nanking of so severe a character that the operation of transferring China to the Sterling Standard could perhaps be accomplished, seeing that the Silver Standard had become too onerous to be endured.

The same line of argument, as it happened, was being pursued by the Masters of Money in the case of the Gold Standard. As has been seen, they had employed all the means at their disposal to prevent France and the other gold countries from devaluing their monies so long as any further deflation of prices in these countries could be brought about. But the time was evidently at hand when deflation by the gold *bloc* must cease. After that the Gold Standard in France could serve no useful purpose, whereas if France elected to link her money to sterling by an act of devaluation which should allow a fixed relationship to be established between franc and pound a great victory over Mr. Roosevelt would have been won.

The disturbed political and economic conditions throughout the world made an excellent battle-field. In America there were strikes and the threat of strikes —notably in the textile industry. In China the pressure of the Communist forces south of Canton kept General Chiang kai-Shek fully occupied and so weakened his influence over the Nanking Government. In

Europe the Nazi pressure against Austria was causing anxiety both in Rome and Paris. In these circumstances the peace and tranquillity of the sterling area seemed to many to afford a true haven of refuge from a hurricane which threatened to destroy the world.

The first shots of the battle were fired early in July when the rise of commodity prices caused by the great drought was occasioning a minor boom in Wall Street and elsewhere. The Silver Lobby became vociferous once more and its demands evoked, immediately, anxious protests from China. Early in August the price of silver, which had been almost stationary for a month, began to rise. After a few days, on August 9th, 1934, Mr. Roosevelt availed himself of the powers which at his request had been granted to him in May. He took possession of the whole of the stock of silver in the United States paying for it at 50·01 cents an ounce. He then issued silver certificates against it, similar to the gold certificates which he had already issued. Private dealings in silver thus became impossible and the opportunities to force up the price were substantially curtailed. A respite to the sorely pressed Chinese Government was thus afforded.

The Masters of Money turned immediately to gold and a boom in that metal began on the London Bullion Market. The effect on the gold *bloc* was immediate and very severe. Europe, indeed, had been in a highly nervous state since the murder of Dr. Dollfuss, the Austrian Chancellor, in Vienna on July 25th with its attendant outbreaks of violence, the death of President von Hindenburg on August 2nd and the consequent assumption of almost absolute power by Herr Hitler. France and Italy, especially, were profoundly uneasy because both countries were well persuaded that Germany had re-armed and was in a bellicose frame of mind. A financial crisis, in such circumstances, is calculated to shake the *moral* of any people.

But great as is the magic of the Masters of Money in the sphere of finance, it lacks sadly where the qualities of the spirit are concerned. No sooner was the idea of a linking of the franc to sterling suggested than every element in the French mind which, during the centuries, has sustained that mind, was awakened to opposition. What? Hand over the control of French monetary policy to London? Opposition to M. Doumergue, who had suggested that the English Political System was better and more flexible than the French, at once began to develop. That fine old patriot stood his ground, demanding the right to dissolve parliament if it obstructed too far, but his arguments were discounted already before he uttered them.

Students of history must have found much to astonish them in M. Doumergue's attitude because the demand that France should adopt English political methods had been made once before. M. Necker, the Swiss Banker who became Treasurer to King Louis XVI and played a part, the importance of which is only now becoming understood, in the destruction of the old French Monarchy, tried in the year 1789 to introduce English Parliamentary methods into France. Then, as now, the suggestion evoked a lively opposition which found its leader in Mirabeau. Mirabeau's question: "Why not introduce also the English language?" stands for all time as the expression of French feeling.

It is impossible not to sympathize with M. Doumergue whose selfless love of country had brought him, reluctantly, from his country home when the streets of Paris were red with Frenchmen's blood. The old man had, clearly, been made the victim of a campaign of "frightfulness". Daily there had been dinned into his ears a tale of the horrors which must be expected—civil war and foreign invasion—if the financial structure of the country was shaken. English methods, in such circumstances, must have seemed the only resource of patriotism.

But Frenchmen have never been careful of their leaders when the honour of France is at stake. As the sterling price of gold began to mount up and the pressure on the franc, in consequence, increased, opposition to abandonment of the Gold Standard at the existing parity in favour of any other standard grew quickly. A Cabinet crisis thus became inevitable.

Meanwhile rumours, like a flock of carrion birds, began to flap over men's heads. France was "coming off gold". China was "coming off silver". War between France and Germany was certain. Japan meant to conquer China. Germany meant to seize Vienna. And so on. Everybody's flesh was made to creep; everybody, somehow, became aware that the way of salvation—the only way—lay in the enlargement of the sterling area to include the whole world. In such circumstances a bare chronicle of facts possesses more worth than any expression of opinion and the reader is referred to Fig. 6 where the course of the sterling prices of gold and silver is shown. The steepest part of the rise in the price of gold took place on the 30th and 31st of August and the 1st of September 1934, three consecutive days, during which the value of the metal increased by some 2*s*. an ounce. On September 1st the great strike in the American textile industry began. In China, on the same day, the Shanghai dollar appreciated sharply in value. This appreciation imposed a strain upon the Chinese economy scarcely less severe than that being imposed by the rising franc upon the French economy. On September 9th the Nanking Government announced that it had been compelled to restrict the sale of foreign exchange. On the 13th violent riots broke out in connexion with the textile strike in the Rhode Island district of the United States. Mr. Roosevelt, however, won the Maine election and thus greatly enhanced his prestige. On the 22nd of September he intervened in the textile strike and settled it.

This rescue of the dollar from immediate danger put new heart into the sorely pressed ranks of the gold and silver *blocs*. But the sterling prices of both metals immediately began to rise once more. The crisis in France was intensified. M. Doumergue continued to press for his new, anglicized political system and so to alienate the sympathy of many of his colleagues who were listening anxiously to the bellicose speeches of the lieutenants of the new Reichschancellor. France is never so unbending as when she is threatened.

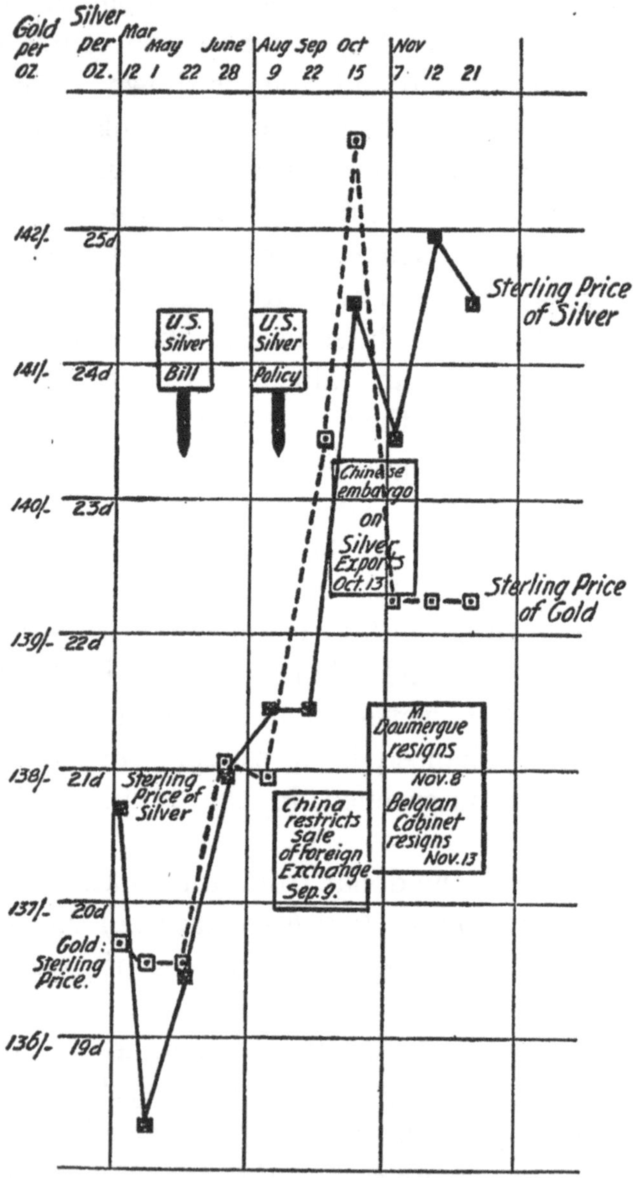

FIG. 6.—FIRST CURRENCY DRIVE.
The course of gold and silver prices in London.

On October 9th, when the sterling price of gold was approaching 143*s.* an ounce (a rise since September 1st of 4*s.* an ounce) and the sterling price of silver was above 2*s.* an ounce (a rise since September 1st of 3*d.* an ounce) an event occurred which, for the moment, drove all other thoughts from men's minds—namely the assassination in the streets of Marseilles of King Alexander of Yugoslavia and M. Barthou, the French Foreign Minister. So great indeed was the horror excited in every country by this dreadful calamity that the political and economic crisis was swallowed up in a far more acute anxiety. Was Europe standing once more on the brink of war? The terrible precedent of Sarajevo was in every mind. Holders of francs made haste to sell them for pounds or dollars and the French Exchange, and with it the sterling price of gold, fell suddenly and violently. But this flight from the franc lasted only a day or two and never, at any time, assumed dangerous proportions. Frenchmen rallied, as of old, to the help of the Fatherland. Within a week the war scare had been discounted.

That scare obscured from many eyes the spectacle presented by China. The Chinese economic crisis, nevertheless, was as severe, in its own way, as the economic crisis in Europe, for all efforts to hold down the exchange value of the Shanghai dollar had proved unavailing in face of the rising price of silver. At the end of September the Nanking Government addressed an urgent plea to President Roosevelt to abandon or suspend his silver policy. That plea was followed by a second and more urgent appeal on October 4th.

The American Government pointed out that the rise in the price of silver was being engineered by forces over which it possessed no control; the silver policy, as such, was not, therefore, the cause of China's distress. Silver meanwhile was standing at about 2*s.* an ounce and the Shanghai dollar had become worth 1*s.* 6*d.* On the 13th October the Nanking Government imposed a 10 per cent duty and equalization charge on silver exports and thus, in a sense, abandoned the Silver Standard. The Shanghai dollar immediately fell about 3*d.* to 1*s.* 3*d.*, and the price of silver declined by 1*d.* an ounce.

On the following day M. Doumergue nominated M. Laval to fill the post made vacant by the murder of M. Barthou. This was a popular appointment because M. Laval held strong nationalist sympathies and France was girded for action. Five days later, in Brussels, France affirmed, before the other members of the gold *bloc*, her determination to maintain the franc at its present gold parity no matter how great the sacrifice necessary to that end might be. All the members of the gold *bloc* pledged themselves to follow the same course.

Neither the gold *bloc*, therefore, nor the silver *bloc*, had submitted to the demands of Money. Each in its own way, on the contrary, had affirmed its independence and upheld its control of its own money. Mr. Roosevelt's great victory in the Congressional elections in November showed his strength to the world and gave grounds for hope that his policy would succeed. The crisis in the French Cabinet immediately became acute once more because France demanded a stronger leadership than M. Doumergue had been able to afford. M. Doumergue resigned and was replaced, as Prime Minister, by M. Flandin. A few days later the Belgian Cabinet also resigned, for similar reasons. The great currency drive was at an end. The Masters of Money had suffered the first serious defeat of the secret war.[1]

[1] France's refusal to devalue made it impossible to raise the sterling price of gold above the point at which the franc tended to " faint ", i.e. to fall against the pound. Because, francs being convertible into gold, the price of the franc in pounds *is* the price of gold in pounds. But if the franc had been devalued this tendency to " fainting " would have been greatly lessened and the sterling price of gold could have been raised once more up to a new " fainting point ". That process of torture must, sooner or later, have induced France to tie her money to sterling. Thereafter there would have been no limit to the possible rise in the sterling price of gold. It would thus have been easy to make the dollar " faint " also and so to force Mr. Roosevelt to devalue or abandon gold. Such abandonment, especially if, in the meantime, China had been brought into the sterling area, would have been equivalent to America's entry into that area.

CHAPTER IX

"FRIGHTFULNESS"

DEFEAT is ruinous to tyrants, because tyrants have no friends. On the morrow of the currency drive the Masters of Money had cause of grave anxiety. Their citadel, the gold *bloc*, belonged to them no more; China, formerly so submissive, refused their demands. The arch-enemy in Washington remained in possession of the field of battle.

Worse still, Mr. Roosevelt was now in a position to afford to the world that focal point of resistance which it had lacked during centuries. France and her allies would inevitably move, in future, towards America, not as towards a master but a friend. The same was true of others among the nations of Europe. It was true, also, to some extent, of China. In each of these countries the forces commanded by the Money Power had been weakened whereas the forces of patriotism and idealism had grown stronger. Governments could be counted upon, henceforward, to resist the demands of bankers and even to wage open warfare upon their bankers.

The Masters of Money were aware, undoubtedly, that they had brought this calamity upon themselves by adopting a plan which cut across national "susceptibilities"—to use their own word. They had not, in the past, been wont to commit so egregious a blunder but needs must when the Devil drives. Deflation, their sovereign weapon, had failed them; the world could not be deflated any more. It had been necessary therefore to use new weapons.

It was still, on the morrow of defeat, necessary to go on using the new weapons seeing that no other means of salvation existed. The Masters of Money, in so far as their minds can be understood from their actions, seem to have convinced themselves that failure had come because the scale of attack had been too small. In the bitter days of November and December 1934 they planned, therefore, a new attack on a scale more nearly in keeping with the seriousness of the issues.

In its strategy this offensive differed but little from its ill-fated predecessor. A Wall Street boom was to upset the price-pattern until the dollar was shaken. The gold *bloc* was to be attacked and driven helter-skelter into the sterling area. China's silver money was to be linked to the pound sterling. So far, however, as tactics were concerned, certain new principles were introduced.

The most important of these was the concentration of the attacking force upon one currency at a time. Another principle was the organization, so far as possible, of opposing groups within the European mass. There was, further, the intention to play off the gold *bloc* against the United States.

The ground in America was prepared with great thoroughness. Mr. Roosevelt's victory at the Congressional elections had been won because the American people loved and trusted him. But, as he was soon to find out, the people's trust does not, infallibly, secure representatives imbued with the people's ideas. Scarcely had the last votes been counted when criticism raised its voice. What, after all, had the President accomplished? Prices had not risen; the mass of unemployment had not sensibly been diminished; thanks to N.R.A. and its codes Big Business was destroying Little Business in every State of the Union, and so on. Again, were all these new laws in strict accord with Washington's Constitution, that sacred writing which every American boy and girl learns by heart? After all, there were Courts before which even the President himself could be brought to answer for his actions. This supposed enemy of "the money changers" moreover was the money changers' best customer. Was he not attempting the impossible task of "borrowing himself out of debt"? Some day the debts would come home to roost.

This propaganda, like the earlier propaganda, enlisted the support of many sincere friends of the Administration, and notably of the large and growing body of monetary reformers who were anxious to see the President "take over the banks" or "nationalize credit". It made doubly difficult, therefore, the task of resisting the boom on Wall Street which had begun in November and was being stimulated in every possible way. Surely the man whose avowed object it was to raise the price-level was not going to put obstacles in the way of those who were fulfilling his behests? Industrial shares began to rise and money to flow into speculation. Would factory prices follow?

The President refused to express any opinion, but his control over speculation became firmer, and his anxiety increased. There was reason for his anxiety. World trade was contracting daily and the French price-level was still falling. Moreover the banking institutions in many countries were offering a stout resistance to Government.[1] On the 25th of November 1934, for example, the Italian Bank Rate had been raised from 4 to 5 per cent, in order to prevent a flight from the lira. This banking measure had been followed, a fortnight later, on December 8th, by an exchange decree which amounted to a mobilization by the Government of foreign balances. In France, too, the banks were showing a great reluctance to come to the help of M. Flandin's administration, which, in consequence, with a national debt of 350,000,000,000 francs on its hands, was approaching a financial crisis. Inflation in America at such a moment could not fail greatly to strengthen the hands of the Money Masters. Signor Mussolini, as it happened, was at that time entering upon his dispute with Abyssinia. The patriotic fervour of the Italian people, in face of a threat of war, exerted an effect upon the banking system which soon proved irresistible. Money was forthcoming for the Government and the Italian price-level rose very sharply (Fig. 7).

The struggle between Government and banks in

[1] Because of the pressure put upon these banking institutions by the Money Masters.

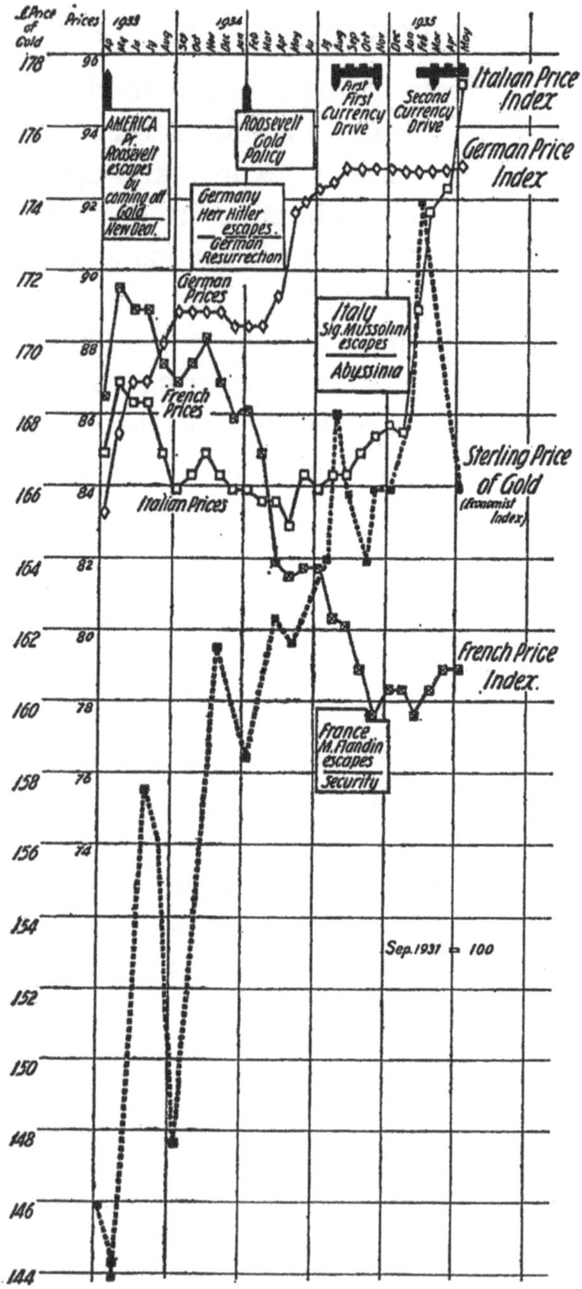

FIG. 7.—THE DEFLATIONARY EFFECT OF THE RISING STERLING PRICE OF GOLD.

Note the warlike methods adopted to escape from deflation.

France was of a more stubborn kind. It continued without special incident until the 2nd of January 1935 when, to the astonishment of the Money Masters, M. Flandin appointed M. Tannery Governor of the Bank of France in place of M. Moret. The occasion was significant in the highest degree because it marked the active revolt of a powerful government against financial dictatorship and revealed the determination to put aside every consideration other than resistance.

Both Herr Hitler and Signor Mussolini had already, before M. Moret's demission, forced their banking systems to lend them money. Reference has already been made to Italy and the Abyssinian question. The German counterpart of that enterprise was the national resurrection as effected by the Nazi party. In both instances the spirit of war was invoked; in both marked success attended the invocation, so much so, indeed, that it can now be accepted as a fact of experience that, when the Masters of Money close down on a government, the way of salvation is immediate appeal to patriotic fervour. There need not necessarily be a war but there must be the sense of danger, of threat, of oppression or of strangulation. Once that feeling has entered men's hearts they are ready to follow their leader anywhere and can no longer be influenced by bankers' propaganda. Bankers, therefore, are compelled to create the necessary credits seeing that, if they should refuse, they would immediately be destroyed.

The story of Fascism and Nazism, indeed, is the

story of a counter-propaganda to Money's propaganda. As the world crisis has grown more and more acute the counter-propaganda has increased in intensity until planning has become discipline and discipline conscription in the face of national emergency. It is not surprising, in these circumstances, that the Masters of Money continue to inveigh against "the Curse of Nationalism".[1]

It is equally, however, without surprise that the leaders of the nations of Europe refuse resolutely to part with the only sure shield they possess against the moneylenders. If Herr Hitler was to disarm completely, Germany would be broken on the signature-money wheel as certainly as night follows day. And the same, exactly, would happen in the case of Italy, if Signor Mussolini relaxed for a day his Fascist propaganda. Finance has made no secret of this and is still, according to its own newspapers, looking forward eagerly to the time when, enthusiasm having died down, budgets will have to be balanced and debts to the creators of signature-money paid.

The historian of the future will, as has been suggested, find much to astonish him in this spectacle of powerful nations, rich in all that men require of goods or services, living in a condition of forced abstinence because certain private persons refused to write their names on little pieces of paper. But if he is a wise

[1] It should be noted, however, that since nationalism of this kind is military it requires the buying of military supplies. Foreign credits have to be used for this purpose and so the difficulty of obtaining Colonial produce is intensified.

historian he will note that in this fact is the final and overwhelming proof of the power and stranglehold of money. It must be true that neither the Italian nor the German dictator was strong enough to cope with the Masters of Money seeing that neither was able, at once, to deliver his people from the paradox of poverty amid plenty, and seeing that deliverance began only when national fervour was opposed to financial obduracy. The Masters of Money, as has been said, made use of the violence of the New Germany to exert pressure on France and Italy, just as they made use of the rising tide of feudalism in Japan to exert pressure on China, but such uses were, essentially, making the best of a bad job. If the currency drive had succeeded and the gold and silver *blocs* had been forced into the sterling area, national fervours would have found themselves opposed not by local banking institutions, upon which pressure could be exerted, but by one single and remote Money Power upon which no pressure of any kind could conceivably have produced any effect. When, therefore, M. Flandin dispensed with the services of M. Moret he was bringing France into the new European system of which Herr Hitler and Signor Mussolini are the chief exponents, and which depends for its future upon the success or failure of the President of the United States.

The Masters of Money have sought to discredit the dictators by posing themselves as the Champions of Democracy and, to some extent, the dictators have helped them in this propaganda by acts of oppression. It should be noted, therefore, that Money's most lively hatred has been reserved not for dictatorship but for the democracy of Mr. Roosevelt. The President of the United States has suppressed no opponents, he has silenced no newspaper, he has held himself obedient in all things to the will of the people. He has not, thus, earned the regard of Wall Street or Lombard Street or the Bourses, where, indeed, prophecy that he will soon be compelled to adopt dictatorial methods, is still as lively as ever. It is not dictatorship which Money hates and it is not democracy which Money desires; the Masters of Money are concerned only to secure that men find and use no other means of exchange than their private signatures. If it be true that, in Europe, military or semi-military dictatorship is the only possible answer to the dictatorship of finance, it is not less true that, once the financial dictatorship has been destroyed, the way will be open again everywhere for democracy.

It is instructive, meanwhile, to observe the course of the French, Italian and German price-levels in their relation to the sterling price of Gold. The Fig. 7 shows that Herr Hitler's coming to power was the signal for an expansion of credit (i.e. larger issue of money) in Germany and that, as power became concentrated more and more in Herr Hitler's hands, money became more and more freely available. The figure shows also that the Italian deflation came to an end soon after Mr. Roosevelt's accession to the Presidency and that a large expansion of credit, and so a sharp rise in the price-level, has attended the Abyssinian dispute. Finally the arrest of the fall in the French price-level which marked the demission from office of M. Moret is clearly shown.[1]

When M. Moret's resignation took place the American price-level had risen substantially and there had been a fairly sharp rise, also, in the price of silver. Congress was just about to meet, and the shouts of the inflationists were already full of menace. In Germany Herr Hitler suddenly called a special meeting of Nazi chiefs; preparations for a Franco-Italian pact were being hurried forward. Europe, in other words, presented the appearance of a hen roost into which a fox is about to enter. Every leader knew that economic "frightfulness" in some form was about to be manifested once more. The question which was uppermost in every mind was: Can Roosevelt ride out the storm? The Money Masters had already assured the world, through the usual channels, that Roosevelt was ruined.

"He has shot his bolt," the story ran. "And he has not got prosperity. Look at the unemployed! Now he is faced with a Congress of Wild Men who are going to take the job of putting things right out of his hands. And you know what that means. Before midsummer the dollar will have gone the way of the mark."

It is curious, in the retrospect, to recall how often the words "before midsummer" were mentioned. One heard them from all sorts of people and in all manner of places. And everyone who spoke them was

[1] The French price-level has since fallen sharply as the result of M. Laval's policy of "consistent deflation", i.e. deflation of debt as well as of prices. But such a fall, *since it reduces debt,* does not reduce total buying-power.

well assured of their truth. Another phrase very commonly used was " the distressing rise of food prices in America ". Nobody, on the other hand, mentioned the fact that the American Price Pattern had been corrected so that farm prices were actually higher than factory prices. This truly wonderful achievement is shown in Fig. 8. Nobody again recalled the fact that the American farmer is the great buyer of American factory goods and that the American export trade amounts only to about 9 per cent of the total American trade. In two years Mr. Roosevelt had changed the conditions out of which the ruin of America had proceeded. It was now only a matter of time until the country regained its prosperity. At long last the Masters of Money had Time for enemy instead of for ally.

Events in the Far East, meanwhile, were marching with events in the West towards the new assault. Japan had already announced that she would view unfavourably any attempt by a foreign power to make a loan to China. As China could not enter the sterling area without a sterling loan, the meaning was obvious. In consequence attacks on Japan began to appear in many newspapers and she was accused of trying to swallow China. This accusation met the retort that " Great Britain seemed to think she ruled all the waves including those of the China Sea ". The *Asahi* newspaper declared, in addition, that Sir Alexander Cadogan, the British Minister in Peking, " was scheming with Mr. Kung, the Chinese Finance Minister, and Mr. Soong against General Chiang kai-Shek and others

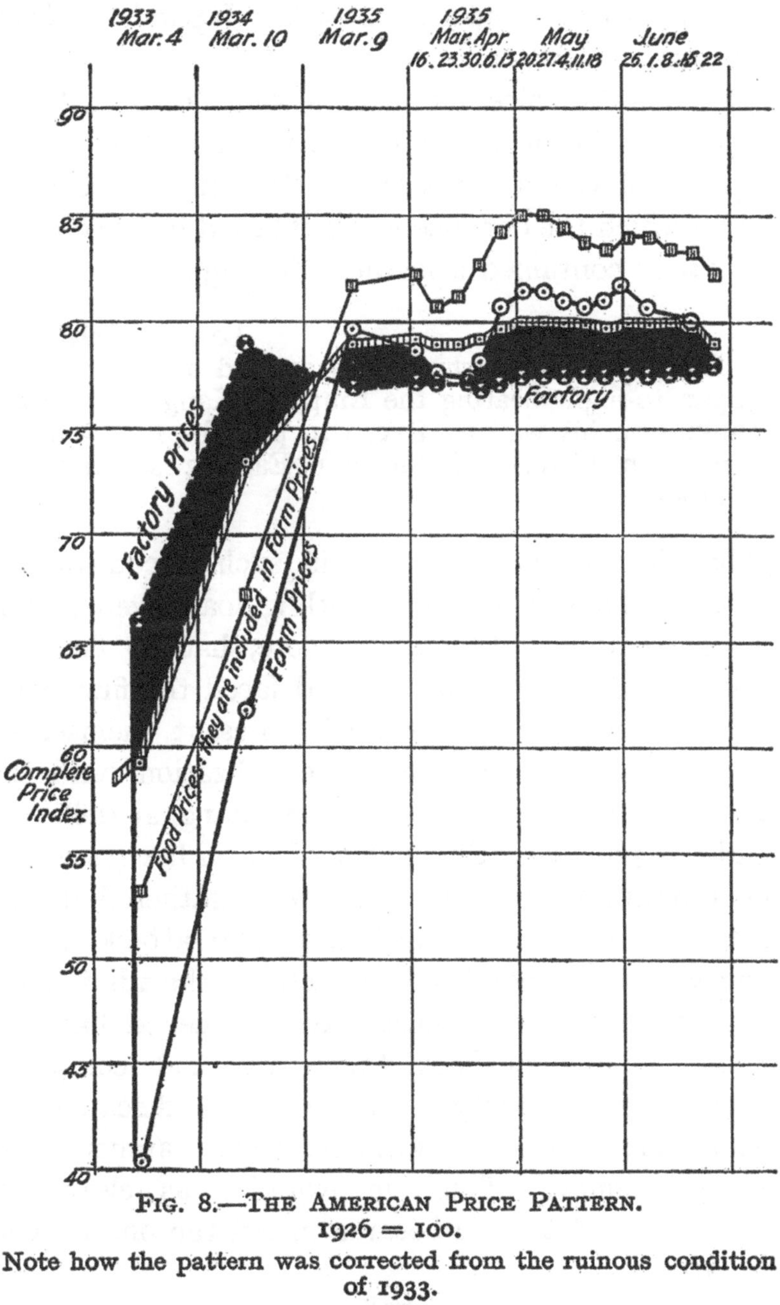

FIG. 8.—THE AMERICAN PRICE PATTERN.
1926 = 100.
Note how the pattern was corrected from the ruinous condition of 1933.

who advocate co-operation with Japan" (*Times*, 6:4:35).

This was the voice not of the Money Power in Japan but of the Army which had made the dispossessed Emperor of China Emperor of Manchukuo. On the day on which the defiance was published in its columns *The Times* contained also the following:

> TOKYO, *April* 6.
>
> The Japanese warship *Hiyei* arrived off the coast of Japan to-night bearing the Emperor Kang Tei of Manchukuo on his way to Tokyo to pay the first visit recorded in history of one Far Eastern sovereign to another.

The Nanking Government, in such circumstances, could not have received a sterling loan even had it wished to do so. China, therefore, had to face the second great offensive as she had faced the first, with such makeshift means as might present themselves. She had, however, set up an equalization fund the object of which was to keep the Shanghai dollar as steady as possible. She had need of all her resources. The Communist armies which were gathered in the South and West had launched a great attack which, in view of the demoralized character of the administrations in these areas, must have succeeded had not General Chiang kai-Shek taken personal command of the Chinese army. The General defeated his opponents; but his operations were hampered by lack of money. Thus, in Nanking as elsewhere, patriotism and finance became pitted the one against the other.

> The presence of the Generalissimo [wrote *The Times* correspondent], intent on a crusade against corrupt officialdom as well as the suppression of Communists, has made a profound impression. . . . These activities of the Generalissimo suggest that great changes are being set in motion and if the spirited attempt to cleanse the Augean stable in the Far West is successful there should be nothing to prevent the application of a similar process in the more sophisticated provinces lying to the East. It is difficult to imagine radical alterations in the thought and conduct of so conservative a people as the Chinese occurring within a short period, but the past year has seen the virtual ruler of this country proceeding by aeroplane accompanied by his wife but without guards or staff and being received with acclamation wherever he goes. He is now directing military operations on a large scale in regions where, twelve months ago, the idea of anything of the kind would have been regarded as fantastically impossible.

See, then, this coming battle not only as Money's last bid for world dictatorship, but also as a first blow struck by patriots for the salvation of the world. The old order is fighting for its life. If defeat is sustained in this encounter, it is likely to be irreparable.

CHAPTER X

FIRST BLOOD

EARLY in January 1935 the opposing forces were aligned for battle. But the intervention of the Supreme Court of the United States prevented action by casting doubts upon the gold value which in the near future the dollar was likely to possess. Until the Supreme Court had given its decision in the so-called " Gold Clause " Case nobody was willing to take the risk of shipping gold to America in exchange for dollars. That outpouring of gold from Europe, upon the effect of which the Masters of Money were basing their hopes, could not therefore take place.

The " Gold Clause " Case dragged on until February 18th, 1935. During the period of respite thus afforded them the world's statesmen made further efforts to protect themselves. M. Flandin and M. Laval, for example, came to London and are said to have urged that England should return to the Gold Standard. This was equivalent to an assurance that France would not enter the sterling area. After the visit, nevertheless, there was an apparent turning of English policy towards France which excited great enthusiasm in Paris.

On February 18th the Supreme Court of the United States decided that it was not incumbent on the

American Government to pay its gold-clause creditors the full amount of their bonds.[1] On the following day the price of gold on the London market began to rise. It continued to rise, slowly, until February 28th when it shot up in less than a week by 5*s.* an ounce.

On March 4th the British Prime Minister issued a memorandum on armaments, in the course of which Herr Hitler was offered some good advice. The memorandum delighted the French, but on the day following its publication Herr Hitler postponed his meeting in Berlin with Sir John Simon. The manner in which this postponement was received in London occasioned both surprise and anger in Paris and the atmosphere of European diplomacy underwent a sharp change. On March 15th, France published her plans for increasing her army; Herr Hitler, the following day, introduced conscription into Germany. The fervour aroused by these nationalist policies served to counteract in the public mind the uneasiness which the economic crisis was producing. It served also as an insurance against weakening by members of the gold *bloc.* But it increased the flight from the franc.

With the single exception of Belgium these stood firm. The attack, therefore, was concentrated upon the Belga which was, notoriously, a weak currency. On March 16th the Belgian Government announced an

[1] Money wanted a Wall Street Boom with rise of factory prices in America. Mr. Roosevelt would then have been faced by a dilemma: 'Shall I allow farmers' prices to fall or raise my price-level by further devaluation of $?' Had he devalued the $ in existing circumstances France would have been driven off gold. Mr. Roosevelt allowed his farmers' prices to fall (Fig. 8).

exchange embargo. Three days later, on the 19th, that Government fell. A shiver of fear ran through France and Holland and Switzerland.

The Masters of Money did not hide their satisfaction which, however, was tempered by slow progress in America. They turned their attention immediately to the Dutch florin and opened a terrific attack on that ancient currency. But the Dutch stood firm and the attack was beaten off. Meanwhile, the Belgian crisis continued and the crisis between France and Germany was intensified. France appealed to the League of Nations against Herr Hitler who, in his turn, refused to admit that he had committed any fault. A bewildered world asked itself if all these marches and counter-marches were play-acting or reality. Those closer to events recognized that both France and Germany were providing against the possibility of France's being forced into the sterling area. If that happened, as Berlin and Paris clearly understood, supplies of money would instantly be cut off unless there was some paramount reason of national security with which to confront the financial powers.

These military fanfares—to which Italy's quarrel with Abyssinia must be added—were exceedingly irksome to the Masters of Money because they increased enormously the difficulty of the task in hand. Was a Germany, a France, an Italy ringing with patriotism and engaged, daily, in military training, going to allow its money to be controlled by foreigners? With ever-deepening anxiety the Masters continued their operations against the Belga and the florin. They had a plan cut and dried and announced it day after day. Belgium was to be the model for all the gold *bloc* countries. Once she had devalued—*on to sterling*—none need fear to take the same course. Unhappily for these bland assurances excitement was being fanned in every European capital. On March 22nd, three weeks after the opening of the offensive, there was a stormy scene in the French Chamber during which England was called the enemy of peace. On the following day Signor Mussolini called up another large batch of conscripts for service in Abyssinia and a most bellicose speech was delivered in Germany by Herr Göring. On the 24th March Dr. Schacht called attention to Germany's desperate financial plight and urged the necessity of conducting trade by barter —that is to say without the use of debt-money. On that day, again, a large number of Italians joined the colours.

Meanwhile, President Roosevelt had been under heavy fire in connexion with his Relief Bill. The bill provided that relief work might be paid at lower wages than the ordinary wages. At once Senator Huey Long raised the cry of "Scab Wages" and began to speak about "the Roosevelt Depression" while Father Couglin, the famous Detroit priest, continued in ever-increasing crescendo to urge his policy of monetary inflation. But on March 24th, while the Belga crisis was at its height, the Relief Bill was passed almost without amendment, an event which did much to encourage the French Government in that it showed the essential strength of Mr. Roosevelt's position. On this day the French Government announced that there was "complete solidarity" with England and Italy as a result of Mr. Eden's visit. The English official announcement, however, spoke of "complete unity of purpose" and the difference was duly noted in Paris and elsewhere.

No Englishman can feel anything but admiration for the heroic efforts made, in these anxious days, by English statesmen to preserve peace and secure disarmament. But it is impossible, at the same time, not to regret that statesmen, generally speaking, remain so ignorant of the aims and methods of the Masters of Money. Obviously neither France nor Germany nor Italy was going to damp down the fervour of its people when such damping down meant an immediate restriction of credit and a terrible financial crisis. As has been said, if the Masters of Money had succeeded in driving the nations of the gold *bloc* into the sterling area and *thus setting up one single form of money for the whole of Europe*, the whole of Europe would have been compelled to make submission. No more nationalism then; no more talk of new deals or national regeneration or national security. Talk, instead, of balanced budgets, of living within one's means, of economy, of retrenchment.

The nations of Europe, like America and China and Japan, were, in short, compelling the Masters of Money to open their purses at a moment when, because of the American resistance to the Debt system, these Masters were determined, above all things, to keep their purses shut. The irreplaceable character of the private-signature-money was being challenged. Its creators and owners were being forced to create more and still more of it and were thus losing that power upon which the whole structure of their system was based—namely, the power to give and take away, the power to raise prices and the power to beat prices down.

If English statesmen had been informed fully about these matters it is obvious that, in their sincere and even passionate quest for peace and disarmament, they would have begun by attacking the real cause of belligerency. Instead of trying to find formulæ or create new pacts which, on pain of fresh deflation and fresh ruin, no nation dared to accept, they would have joined forces with America and asserted, with her, the sovereign right of nations to issue and control their means of exchange. They would, thus, have put an end to the ghastly farce whereby the only means of obtaining money was war or the rumour of war, and to the still more ghastly farce whereby millions were compelled to starve for want of a few scraps of dirty paper bearing the signature of a few more or less indigent old gentlemen who by the exercise of an infinite cunning had turned these signatures into the money of mankind.

Unhappily, the ignorance of money matters which characterizes so many Englishmen, gave to English policy, in this hour of battle, an appearance of insincerity and even callousness, which aroused the contempt of many nations. Thus the English passion for peace was transmuted, in the minds of sorely pressed peoples, into a cool indifference to their troubles. In a few cases, indeed, England was accused of being in secret alliance with the Masters of Money. Were not the sterling price of gold and the sterling price of silver the terrible weapons by which West and East were being punished?

No Englishman, who is able to dissociate international finance from its world centre, or who can see clearly the difference between the so-called "City" of London and the Capital of the British Empire, imagines for a moment that the English people or their Government were acting, in these critical days, from other than sincere motives. The English people suffered in the Great War so terribly that, if it had not been peace-loving formerly, it must have become peace-loving as a result of that ordeal. There is in England to-day a passion for peace and a hatred of war which springs from the souls of the people and is the expression of the deepest of their feelings. It is that passion which has informed and animated English statesmen.

But the outside world, which, necessarily, looks only at the surface of English life, is apt to associate the "world's financial centre" with the people upon whom so many of the Masters of Money are quartered. Because the English people have allowed their excellent mechanism of trade to be used by all comers, that mechanism, distorted into an engine of destruction, has been regarded as the expression of England's perfidy.

Nor is it easy to blame the French or the Germans or the Italians for this mistake. Each time, as has been seen, that the Masters of Money attempted to drive the Continental nations towards the sterling area, resistance in the form of sabre-rattling and nationalist heroics broke out all over Europe—that kind of resistance being the only kind which offered the smallest hope of success. Herr Hitler and his lieutenants, for example, would affirm once more the ancient truths of the Old Germany and would speak in menacing tones of the humiliations of Versailles. "Shall men, shall *money* be lacking to uphold the New Germany?" Eagerly snatching at this occasion of fervour, Messrs. Flandin and Laval would declare that France must be ready to defend her sacred soil no matter at what cost of men *or money*. Signor Mussolini, thereupon, would inform Italy and Europe once more about the destiny of "the Great Nation", fulfilment of which must necessarily cost *a great deal of money*.

English statesmen, while these pyrotechnic displays were going on, habitually, as has been seen, became greatly alarmed, because they did not read correctly the meaning of the speeches. Was Germany going to attack France? Was France going to attack Germany? Was Russia going to attack Germany? And so on. In consequence hurried visits to European capitals by English Ministers invariably occurred while currency drives were in progress. Not unnaturally, therefore, the pilgrimages and the currency drives became associated in French and German and Italian minds. Thus the cause of peace received less support than it would have done had knowledge of money and its methods been more extensive.

On the 24th of March 1935, when the Belgian crisis was still at its height, Sir John Simon and Mr. Eden reached Berlin to confer with Herr Hitler about peace. These conferences were in progress when the decision to devalue the belga was taken and when, in consequence, it became obvious that Belgium was about to enter the sterling area. In such circumstances of anxiety for Germany and France, the wisest counsels in the world were likely to fall on deaf ears.

Meanwhile the Wall Street boom was sagging and American farm prices had begun to rise again. Money was flowing back to the commodity markets. On the 28th of March M. van Zeeland, the new Belgian Premier, formally devalued the belga by some 25 to 30 per cent and that currency was received—more or less—into the sterling area. In other words a relationship was established between the belga and the pound sterling. On the 30th the Belgian Chamber ratified this devaluation.

Instantly France reasserted her sovereignty and reaffirmed her determination never, in any circumstances, to depart from the existing gold parity of the franc. M. Flandin, indeed, declared that he would mint gold francs and put them into the hands of the people, a serious threat to the Masters of Money who had taken gold, everywhere, out of the peoples hands in order to keep it under their own control. People in possession of gold, or able to obtain gold on demand from the Masters of Money, are less easy to deal with than people who do not enjoy these rights.

In spite of M. Flandin's boldness, however, the gold

currencies remained exceedingly weak and there were "runs" on the Dutch, Swiss and French banks and heavy exports of gold to America and London. On April 6th, however, Belgium made a commercial agreement with France whereby she pledged herself not to sell in France, by means of her devalued money, below French prices—a sign that France had brought such strong pressure to bear upon her as almost to take her bodily out of the sterling area into which she had just entered. This Franco-Belgian agreement warned the world that France would resist to the utmost the demands of the Masters of Money and for a day or two steadied the exchanges. On the 16th of April, however, a new and most violent attack was made upon the Dutch florin. The Dutch Bank Rate, which had been raised already from 2½ per cent to 3½ per cent, was raised further to 4½ per cent. On that day, in the United States, Mr. Roosevelt's train was nearly wrecked by a motor-car which had been abandoned on a level crossing at the moment when the train was approaching. This danger, happily, was obviated by the watchfulness of the engine-driver.

Meanwhile, in China, the drive against the Shanghai dollar had been of an exceedingly severe character. The pressure exerted by the Communists in the south has already been referred to. It had been relieved to some extent by the brilliant leadership of Chiang kai-Shek but remained a serious source of anxiety. Chiang kai-Shek, on the other hand, could and did make use of it, in the manner of the European dictators, to demand plentiful supplies of *money*. Thus, in China, the same kind of pressure was being exerted on the Masters of Money as was being exerted in Europe. In Japan, too, national fervour, awakened by the march of the army to the Great Wall of China, was causing the banks to expand credit and raise the level of prices. The Sino-Japanese quarrel, like the Franco-German quarrel was, thus, of the utmost advantage and importance both to the Chinese and Japanese Governments—or at any rate to those elements in the Chinese and Japanese Governments which were not closely allied to the financial interests. In the circumstances, the efforts of the League of Nations to find formulæ of agreement for the contestants partook of the same weakness as the efforts of the British Government to find formulæ in Europe and caused Japanese statesmen to suggest that the League of Nations was acting in the interests of Money.

The sharp rise in the sterling price of silver which, as has been seen, had occurred coincidently with the rise in the sterling price of gold, was accompanied, therefore, by bellicose speeches both in China and in Japan, in which the need for heavy expenditure upon national safety and national glory was stressed. On March 21st, Mr. H. H. Kung, the Finance Minister of the Nanking Government, announced that his Government had

> received a communication from Britain asking for opinion on a plan for relieving the financial situation in China. The British Government also, said Mr. Kung, expressed its willingness to co-operate with other powers interested with a view to extending effective assistance to China. (Reuter: quoted by the *Financial News*, 22nd March 1935.)

This offer was not accepted. On the contrary, the Chinese Government issued $100,000,000 of domestic bonds for the purpose of increasing the capital of the Central Bank of China, the Bank of China and the Bank of Communications. This was open defiance of the Money Power and sent a thrill of excitement through the world because it meant that the Nationalist leaders had forced the Government to serve their purposes. China was set upon the way which Germany and Italy and France were now pursuing. A writer in *The Times*, discussing this step on June 28th, said:

> Fear of future developments has affected public confidence, and it is surprising that the (Nanking) Government has risked an access of this feeling by arbitrarily taking over control of the Bank of China and the Bank of Communications, both registered companies in which the Government had only a small holding. . . .
>
> This manœuvre startled all the Chinese banks since it shows that the Government is prepared, when it thinks fit, to take control of their affairs and of their resources regardless of the wishes of the shareholders. The Chinese banks, it should be said, have been the mainstay of the National Government since its establishment, supporting loan issues and making advances to meet requirements. The banks have lately become, for obvious reasons, decidedly cautious about additional financing, but have been unable to avoid complying with the demands made upon them. It was the banks that stood out for official assurances that there was no intention to devalue the currency or to adopt some kindred expedient and the fact that the Government has now assumed control of two of the biggest of these institutions . . . has been interpreted as showing the intention of the Government to pursue an independent financial policy untrammelled by opposition.

That interpretation was the right one. As the

smugglers made away with China's silver and the "speculators" forced up the sterling price of the metal, the Chinese Government *replaced* the vanishing credit by new money of its own creation and so saved the country from ruin. The prospect that China might enter the sterling area now became exceedingly remote and there were rumours, early in April, that Japan might leave the sterling area and link the yen to the dollar.

So far, therefore, the Masters of Money had achieved nothing except the devaluation of the belga and the rather doubtful adherence of that currency to sterling. The position was growing desperate. A new assault was immediately launched.

CHAPTER XI

THE DAY OF JUNE 6TH, 1935

THIS second assault of the Second Currency Drive was designed to raise the price of silver and to depress the price of gold—thus reducing the ratio between gold and silver and imposing upon the Chinese export trade, and so upon the Chinese exchequer, a burden of the utmost severity.

The Fig. 9 shows how thoroughly the plan was carried out. Between April 1st and April 27th, 1935, the sterling price of silver rose about 8*d*. an ounce, while the price of gold continued to fall. Thus the ratio between silver and gold moved from about 62 : 1 to about 40 : 1.

A new financial crisis immediately began in Shanghai, where, in spite of the efforts to hold it down, the Chinese dollar was increasing in value. Representations were addressed to Washington, but Mr. Roosevelt found himself in the difficulty that he had promised to buy silver mined in the United States at world prices so that there might be no loss to the American silver interests. When, therefore, on April 10th the price of silver rose above 64½ cents an ounce the President had to reduce his minting charge from 50 per cent to 45 per cent and so raise his silver-buying price to

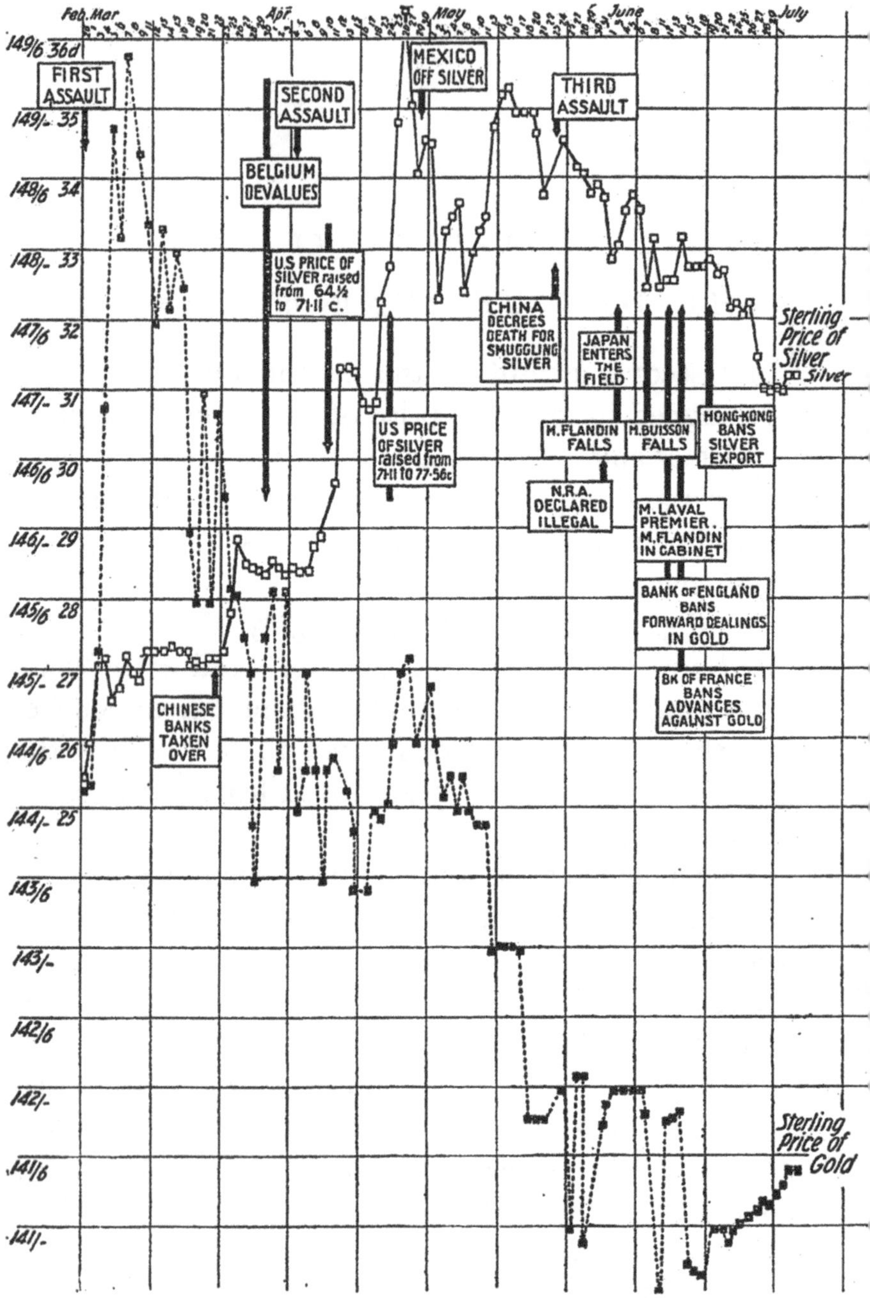

FIG. 9.—THE SECOND CURRENCY DRIVE.
Note the three separate assaults.

71·11 cents an ounce. On the 24th April a second reduction of minting charge (45 per cent to 40 per cent) became necessary and the price rose to 77·56 cents an ounce. The sterling price of silver immediately passed the 3*s*. an ounce mark.[1]

It was now confidently predicted that the American price would be forced up to $1 an ounce and that China would be forced to " come off " and seek safety in the sterling area. But on April 27th all the banks in Mexico City were closed. Mexico abandoned the Silver Standard and announced her intention of entering the dollar area. That news, with its suggestion that large quantities of silver might soon appear on the market, broke the boom and the price of silver fell in a few days to 2*s*. 8*d*. an ounce.

This was blessed relief to the Chinese Government. Taken in conjunction with the fact that the Canadian Government had announced a " New Deal " and begun, earlier in April, to mint silver coins—thus promising a fixed price for silver—it was relief also for Mr. Roosevelt, whose hand, in the matter of the price of silver, could no longer be forced. Further there was the spectacle of a dollar-area extending from the Hudson Bay to the Gulf of Mexico. But who shall blame Canada? At that very moment " the City " was ringing with angry cries against the Government of Ontario, which, in sheer desperation, was threatening to reduce the payments on some of its loans.

Unhappily the strain on China was soon renewed. Silver began to rise again on the 9th of May and by

[1] Carrying up with it the English price-level.

the 15th was standing above *2s. 11d.* an ounce, while gold had fallen steeply from about 145*s.* an ounce to 143*s.* The ratio between silver and gold was, therefore, still about 40 : 1.

On May the 13th, while this second rise was in progress Mr. Morgenthau, the Secretary of the United States Treasury, delivered a wireless address to the whole American people in which he indulged in some plain speaking about the Masters of Money. He said:

> The citizenship of these snipers is not important since their dominant trait is an utter lack of patriotism and loyalty to any nation. They would sell civilization "short" if they could.

This speech did not promise any strong action about silver and the price of the metal began to fall once more and continued to fall, day after day, until on June 30th the price had reached *2s. 7d.* an ounce. The price of gold meanwhile had fallen to 141*s.* an ounce and the ratio had risen, therefore, to about 45 : 1. On May 14th Italy placed an embargo on silver exports in order to protect her currency.

Meanwhile, in China, this prolonged and terrible strain had coincided in point of time with a series of brilliant operations by General Chiang kai-Shek against the Communists of the South and West and with, in consequence, an outburst of Nationalist feeling. This outburst secured the supply of money and silenced the voices that were raised in favour of a sterling loan. It had its repercussions, too, in Tokyo where, without consulting the Japanese Army leaders, the Government raised the Legation in China to an

Embassy—a course which was followed by England and other countries. On May 21st the Chinese Government at Nanking announced that it would visit with the penalty of death the smuggling of silver out of China "as a crime menacing the safety of the Republic". The price of silver, which had been expected to rise to 4*s.* or even 5*s.* an ounce, was sagging downwards at 2*s.* 10*d.* an ounce. The second assault had ended, as the first had ended, in most ignominious defeat.

But defeat must somehow be turned into victory, even yet, at this eleventh hour. As the beaten forces of the second assault straggled backwards, a third assault, this time upon both the gold and silver fronts, was launched with the reckless violence of despair. Strategy in this instance was based upon the maintenance of as high a silver price as possible, in association with a relatively low price for gold. In other words China was to be held under as great a strain as possible while the smugglers across the border in Korea and elsewhere continued their disastrous work; the gold *bloc* on the other hand was to be subjected to a "run" which must have the effect of bringing Governments and banking systems into sharp conflict.

In the East this plan broke down owing to the sudden and dramatic appearance of Japan. On May 30th the Japanese Military Authorities in North China presented a number of demands to the Chinese Government in connexion with alleged anti-Japanese activities in the demilitarized zone south of the Great Wall. These demands were not very vigorously pressed and on

June 6th it was announced that "Sino-Japanese authorities will shortly take joint measures to suppress the drug traffic in the demilitarized zone". Smuggling was not mentioned but was clearly in mind. On June 9th the Japanese Army demanded, further, the abolition of the Peking Political Council and other bodies. On June 12th in response to a report from Paris that it was proposed to hold an international conference in Nanking to consider China's financial position, the Japanese Foreign Office informed the vernacular press that Japan would not take part, as such a conference would be conducive to placing China under international supervision.

The Japanese demands were agreed to by China. Meanwhile, on June 25th *The Times* correspondent wrote:

> PEKING.
>
> Over 600,000 silver dollars have been brought to Peking from Shanghai to alleviate the financial crisis among the Chinese banks. The crisis has been aggravated by the steady outflow of silver dollars from North China.
>
> Chinese smugglers are liable to the death penalty but the police find it difficult to deal effectively with the numbers of Koreans engaged in the organized export of silver dollars to Manchukuo.
>
> Koreans are also active in the illicit drug traffic in the demilitarized zone.

On June 3rd Reuter's correspondent in Shanghai wrote:

> Another crisis due to America's dear silver policy which threatened to engulf many of the smaller Chinese banks has been averted by the action of the Ministry

of Finance. The Minister has advanced $25,000,000 (Chinese) of Government bonds against securities of twice that amount put up by the Chinese Bankers' Guild, to firms which are solvent but temporarily embarrassed. . . .

It is estimated that about 300,000,000 ounces of silver have been shipped out of China since the American Silver Purchase Act became operative, with serious results to trade and commerce. . . . There is believed to be much smuggling. . . .

On June 12th it was announced that the British Government would shortly send its chief economic adviser to China to study conditions and report. It was further announced that Hong Kong had decided to place an embargo on the export of silver to take effect from June 15th. This, in the words of the *Financial News*, was "a gesture of co-operation with China". Englishmen may reasonably regret that the gesture had not been made somewhat earlier before the Chinese Government emerged a victor from its struggle. A study of all these facts suggest that the Japanese intervention, whatever its other aims may have been, had the effect of relieving the pressure on the Chinese banks caused by the smuggling of silver. It, thus, had the effect of hampering the third assault of the Money Power so far as the Orient was concerned. But in the West that assault met with no such unexpected obstacle.

The Western strategy was based upon the cross-rate between the dollar and the franc, that is to say on the difference in price existing between these two monies. If the dollar is "strong" while the franc is "weak" then it will pay to take francs to the Bank of France, demand gold for them and, with the gold, buy dollars. In other words, until the franc strengthens again there will be a run on the Bank of France. And if, in addition, a better price is obtainable for gold in London than in Paris, a drain of gold to London will also take place (see Fig. 10).

On May 20th, the franc weakened sharply against the dollar, as the result of a heavy buying of dollars with francs—that is to say of a heavy selling of francs. Gold at once began to pour out of the Bank of France. At the same time, although the sterling price of gold did not rise, very active buying in London caused the " premium " over the franc to increase from about *2d.* an ounce to *2s. 7d.* an ounce. (This means that, whereas gold could have been bought in Paris at less than 140*s.* an ounce people in London were prepared to pay more than 142*s.* an ounce for it.) In such circumstances owners of francs cash them and bring the gold to London in order to obtain " the premium ". Here is another occasion of what the French have called, wittily, " bleeding " a bank of its gold.

Not unnaturally the Regents of the Bank of France tried to protect themselves against this monetary phlebotomy by raising the bank rate and refusing to lend. But the policy of M. Flandin's Government depended on cheap money and easy borrowing. Thus Government and Central Bank were thrown at once into acute conflict. It was a conflict of a very bitter kind because there were reports that the Governor of the Netherlands Bank was now in favour of devalua-

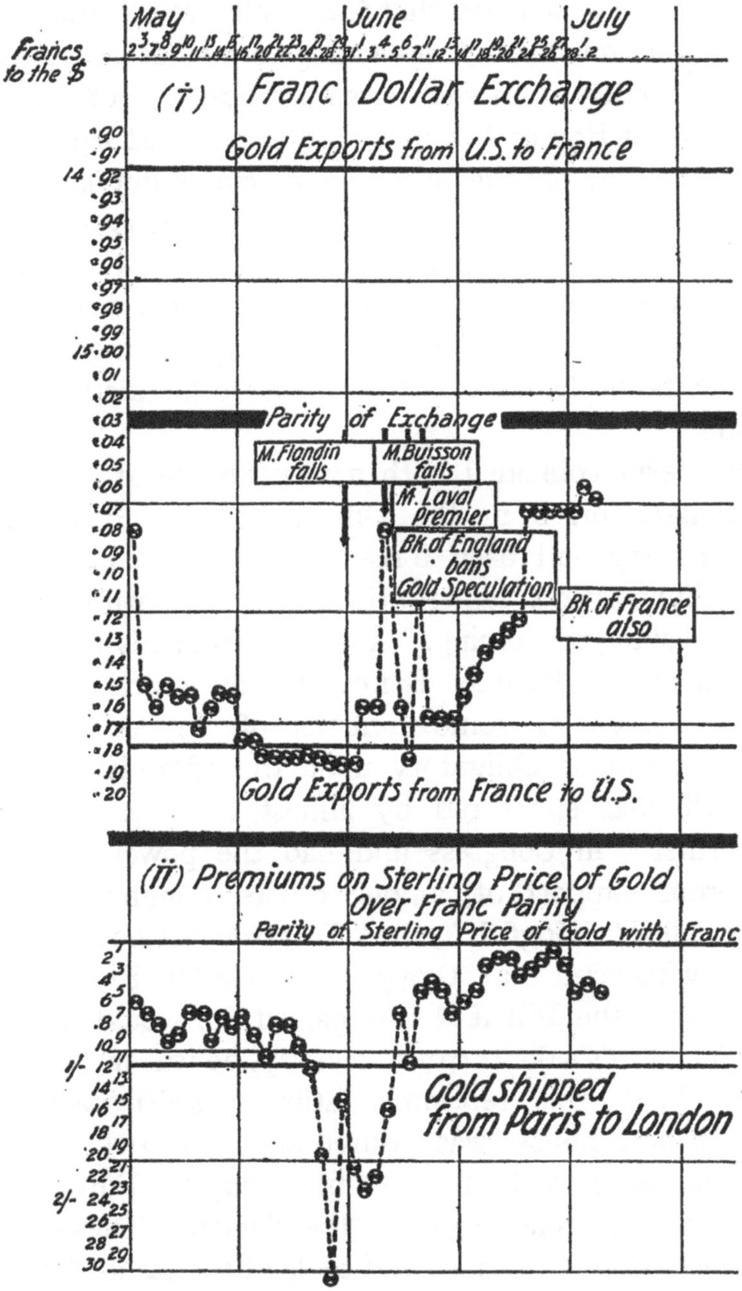

FIG. 10.—FRANCE LOSES GOLD.

tion and it was believed that the coming referendum in Switzerland must result in a change of monetary policy in that country. In such circumstances the rulers of the Bank of France felt bound to exert great caution.

M. Flandin, on the other hand, could not govern without money. As it happened he was very unwell because he had broken his arm when a car that was being backed out of a garage had collided with his car a few days before. He had to postpone, therefore, his inevitable demand to the Chamber for dictatorial powers.

The delay coincided with a new and most violent inflationary drive in the United States. Prices in that country had been forced up sharply, amid the usual hypocritical lamentations of those who were accomplishing the forcing. Attention suddenly became focused on the Patman Bonus Bill by which an immediate issue of some millions of "greenbacks" was to be made obligatory upon the administration. The Bill was sponsored by almost every monetary "reformer" in Congress and had the powerful and vociferous support of, among others, Senator Huey Long, called "Kingfish", the "Dictator" of Louisiana. It was whispered that, though of course Mr. Roosevelt would veto the Bill if it was passed, he would do so only for form's sake because, secretly, he was in favour of it. With this recommendation a swift passage through both houses was assured and duly took place. Mr. Roosevelt, with his eyes fixed on the European and Oriental scenes saw all the danger. These inflationists were the dupes and tools of the same Power which was rending China and devouring the countries of the Old World. If the dollar was destroyed resistance to the Masters of Money must, everywhere, collapse. Then the world would have only one money, issued from one centre and there would be no people on earth powerful enough by any exercise of war fever or patriotic frenzy to compel the issue of a single farthing which the Masters of the One Money did not wish to disburse.

Mr. Roosevelt, as his action shows, understood that what was at stake in those days of May was not an American Bill but the fate of the world. The Masters of Money, in their extremity, were playing high; since they could not have their signature-money based on gold as of yore, they would show the nations that their money was to be preferred to gold. Let Mr. Roosevelt keep his gold; it would turn, soon, to dross in his hands. The sterling area should be stretched once more as in the Nineteenth Century to encompass the world and they would reign once more over the sterling area.

Let none dismiss this picture as a dream, and least of all any Englishman. The stage, only a few months ago, was set; hopes were ripening into convictions so that, already, plans were being made for the reception and division of the spoil. Patriotism, nationalism, freedom—all were marked down for an early destruction. In their place was to stand an universal subservience, slavery without appeal. . . .

The President of the United States went in person to Parliament and, in stern voice, denounced the Bill that must ruin the world. Half an hour later the House of Representatives passed the Bill by an overwhelming majority. But on the next day the Senate rejected it, narrowly and grudgingly.

Salvation had come only just in time. On May 25th, a Saturday, a terrific attack on the franc took place and huge withdrawals of gold were made from the Bank of France. Panic spread, immediately, over the face of Europe producing its accustomed crop of bellicose speeches. Sunday 26th, in consequence, was a day of anxious comings and goings, but no promise of relief could anywhere be obtained. On Monday, 27th May, the attack on the franc was renewed and the blood-letting of gold spread to Switzerland and Holland. And then, suddenly, it became known that the Supreme Court of the United States had declared the basis of the " New Deal ", N.R.A., an illegal measure.

That news shook " the world ". In America the inflated prices came tumbling down and the dollar fell against the franc. Those who had been " bulling " the markets fled for cover. The strain on the franc was momentarily eased. Next morning, the 29th, there was a sudden change of opinion. The fall of N.R.A. had destroyed the hope of inflating the U.S. price-level and so ruining the dollar. Further, it had brought again into operation Mr. Theodore Roosevelt's anti-trust laws which N.R.A. had suspended.

The attack on the franc, nevertheless, went on with ever-growing violence. M. Flandin announced his readiness to come to the Chamber and fight his battle. He came, with his broken arm in a sling. In tones of grave warning he told his fellow countrymen that the decision they were about to take concerned not the franc only but France. A spate of deflationary oratory from the currency reformers who, here as in America, were showing themselves incapable of distinguishing friend from foe, washed his words away. He did not hear the oratory because he had fainted. But the Chamber refused him the dictatorial powers he had asked for. Before morning the Flandin Ministry had fallen.

It was victory for the Masters of Money. A shout of jubilation went up in all the "cities" and "bourses". Now, at last, the way was clear to the goal, for where France led there Switzerland and Holland and Italy and Germany must follow. The franc-dollar exchange recovered as if by magic and the high premium being paid on gold in London melted away. It was announced that M. Bouisson had formed a Ministry with M. Caillaux as his Finance Minister.

Suddenly there was a chill. M. Caillaux, too, it seemed believed that the franc ought to remain on gold. Jubilation gave place to a new anxiety and once again the exchanges weakened. M. Bouisson asked for dictatorial powers just as M. Flandin had asked. His government, like M. Flandin's government, was driven from office, though by a very narrow majority.

It was now trumpeted abroad that France would not be able to find a government until the demands of the Masters of Money were granted. The President of the Republic sent for M. Laval; but he begged to be excused. Then for M. Pietri. Then again for M. Laval. Late on the night of June 6th the man who had been M. Flandin's Foreign Minister and Chief Lieutenant became Prime Minister of France. And M. Flandin was a member of his Cabinet. The battle was won. On this occasion the Chamber voted the dictatorial powers which, formerly, it had refused.

On June 8th, the day following M. Laval's entry into office, the Bank of England addressed a circular to all London banks and bullion brokers requesting them to refrain from accepting orders for forward dealings in gold on account of speculation. The *Financial News* commented:

> The object of this move is to discourage speculation against gold currencies. Ever since the forward market in gold has developed during the last few years, a large part of its transactions has consisted of buying forward gold against francs or some other gold currency. . . . The existence of such facilities encouraged speculative selling of gold currencies and was therefore partially responsible for the bear attacks. It is in order to protect the franc against such attacks that the Bank of England has decided to use its influence in the London Market to put an end to the practice.

The Bank of England in other words closed the doors of the sterling markets against the Masters of Money by warning all bankers to avoid giving services to "speculators" in forward gold. That "Big Bad Wolf" the sterling price of gold, which during four years had vexed all the countries of the West, was taken by the throat at last. Henceforward the sterling price of gold with its premiums would be made to serve the purposes of trade.

Few, perhaps, of those who read the bald statement about the Bank's circular in the morning papers realized that they were reading the death-notice of an epoch. The Bank of England had defied the Money Power. The Bank of England had warned off those nameless Masters of Money at whose threat, even a few days before, every banking institution on earth had trembled. "*Le roi est mort.*"

Nor was the Bank of England alone in this defiance: On June 11th the Bank of France announced that it would suspend further advances against gold with a view to checking speculation. Thus the English and French Treasuries and their Central Banks stood side by side against the common enemy. England, too, had escaped out of that universal sterling area into which the Masters of Money had sought to force her. England was on her way back to gold, the automatic Gold Standard with its silver pendulum which Mr. Roosevelt had given to the world. The resistance offered long ago by Mr. Joseph Chamberlain and Mr. Lloyd George to the foreign-loan Gold Standard was justified in the ruin of the plan for a Universal Debt Money.

How little this was understood by most Englishmen can be inferred from many of the newspaper comments on the Bank of England's circular. A writer in the *Financial News*, for example, said:

> Apart altogether from the question whether it is to the advantage of France to encourage her leaders to continue their deflationary policy, it may well be asked whether, even from a strictly orthodox point of view, this inadequate result will be worth the sacrifice involved. For the embargo on foreign gold operations

will result in a very real loss from the view-point of London's rôle as an international banking centre, a loss which the banking community will have every reason to deplore. The development of a forward market in gold since the crisis compensated London to an appreciable extent for the decline of the international importance of her acceptance credit and discount market. It added to the unique technical facilities of London as a banking centre. . . .

The embargo on forward dealing in gold came as a surprise since it has never been supposed that Whitehall would look particularly askance at a devaluation of the remaining gold currencies. It is recognized that this would simplify the international currency situation and pave the way for an eventual solution of the monetary problem. Hitherto the official attitude has been one of absolute neutrality as regards the struggles of the gold *bloc*. The Equalization Account has certainly been used to smooth out the downward movements in the franc, but there has been no hint of any positive assistance to safeguard the franc's permanent stability.

In the circumstances this new step is distinctly unexpected and almost amounts to a perceptible change of policy. There often seems to be a certain difference between the Treasury's attitude and the Bank of England's attitude on various matters, and in this case no doubt the initiative came from the Bank of England. Gold Standard Stability is evidently put on a lower pedestal in Whitehall than it is in Threadneedle Street where importance is no doubt attached to the general principle of protecting a gold currency as far as possible from speculative attack.

This writer may have changed some, at any rate, of his views when he read the speech of the Governor of the Bank of France, M. Jean Tannery, at Basle on June 16th. M. Tannery said:

While in April and during the first week of May withdrawals did not exceed 60,000,000 francs a day, they increased to 85,000,000 francs in the second week, to 500,000,000 francs in the third and to 1,000,000,000 francs in the fourth. The total sum of withdrawals from May 4th to June 7th amounted to 9,900,000,000 francs, half of which went to the United States, the other half remaining in Europe. The Banque de France reacted vigorously: first by raising the discount rate from 2½ to 6 per cent; and secondly by an active control of exchange movements in order to maintain the free circulation of gold.

M. Tannery here said he recognized the great importance of the assistance given by the American Treasury Department, thanks to the understanding of Mr. Morgenthau who supplied the market abundantly with dollars to prevent the dangerous consequences of a sudden stoppage of gold purchases.

A third measure taken by the bank (of France) was strong credit restrictions imposed on the banks. This policy had been supported by the spontaneous intervention of the Bank of England (*Times*, 17/6/35).

Mr. Morgenthau was asked about the help he had given. He described it as " common decency between nations ". It was that, and much more. In the latter days of this great battle America and England were standing together beside France and it was, therefore, by the united efforts of the three great democracies that the Masters of Money and their legions were brought, on June 6th, when M. Laval accepted the Premiership, to irretrievable defeat and ruin.

CHAPTER XII

ROUT

IT is now, one month after the rout of the Masters of Money in their greatest battle, certain that the defeat is irreparable. The Money Power has been destroyed and the Credit or Debt System must very soon disappear from the world.[1]

This becomes obvious when it is realized that the architects of the Gold Standard in its foreign-loan form were, on March 1st, when Money's Armageddon began, taking the field against gold in favour of sterling because the world's stocks of the yellow metal no longer belonged to them, and because, therefore, their supreme weapon rested in the hands of their enemies. By taking possession of more than half the gold in the world, as the representative of the American people, President Roosevelt had made a gold basis of private-signature-money an impossibility. France's resistance to entry into the sterling area had placed nearly the whole of the remaining gold stock beyond the reach of the Masters of Money. Finally, Mr. Roosevelt's silver pendulum had secured that the automatic action of the

[1] September 20th.—In the months which have elapsed since this opinion was expressed its validity has remained unchallenged.

international Gold Standard would never again be prevented by foreign loans.

The great battle was fought, primarily, to replace gold, as the basis of credit, by sterling and to make of

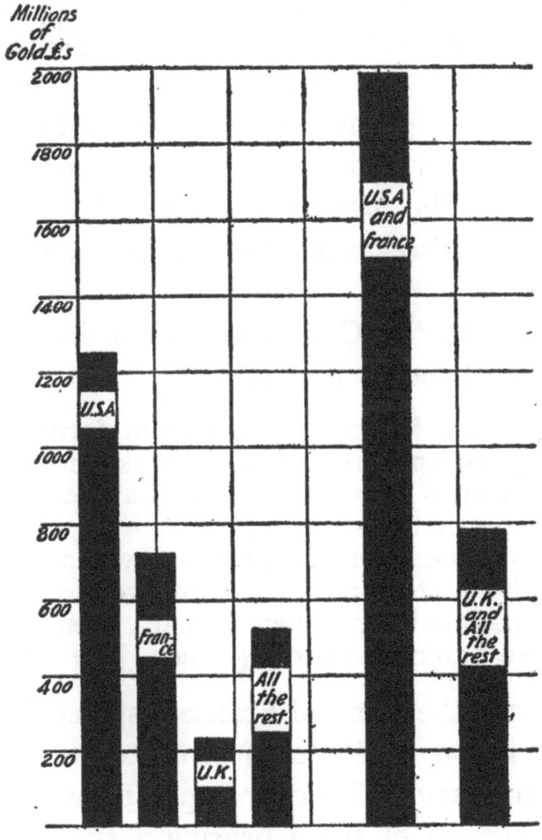

FIG. 11.—GOLD STOCKS, 1935.

silver once more a mere base metal. At the end of the battle gold and silver remained the bases of the world's monetary structure and had passed, almost entirely, into the possession of the world's governments (Fig. 11).

Again the battle was fought to link national currencies to an international signature-money based on sterling. At its end national currencies remained national, with no other link than the precious metals between them.

The battle was fought, further, to prevent the stabilization of the pound sterling on gold so that the sterling price of gold might continue to be used as a battering-ram against the gold currencies. On the morrow of victory the use of this weapon was denied absolutely to the Masters of Money by the Bank of England and also, in another direction, by the Bank of France.

On July 7th the Governors of the Bank of International Settlements at Basle

> agreed to join in common action in future as soon as the first sign appeared of any attack on the currencies of the countries represented in the Bank of International Settlements in the same way as it was possible to stop the recent attacks on the French, Swiss and Dutch currencies thanks to the common intervention of the Bank of International Settlements board members in their respective banking centres (*Times*, July 8th, 1935).

On July 10th the Bank of France instructed the Bankers' Association in Paris to limit to what might be strictly necessary " all forward operations on exchanges to the exclusion of those bearing a speculative character ". A similar order was issued about the same time by the Bank of the Netherlands.

The Federal Reserve Board, meanwhile, announced in New York on July 4th that " arrangements were made on November 28th, 1934, to advance up to $50,000,000, to be secured by gold, to assist the gold *bloc* countries ". No use of the credit was made " last year ". Earlier in November an advance of $25,000,000 was made to the National Bank of Belgium.

On July 7th the U.S. Treasury borrowed £100,000,000 for five years and five months at the rate of 1⅜ per cent—a low rate without any precedent. The issue was subscribed more than three times over. The U.S. budget deficit which had been expected to amount to nearly £1,000,000,000 was returned at £700,000,000.

On July 9th the Austrian bank-rate was reduced from 4 to 3½ and reductions followed in the French and Dutch bank-rates.

An assault which fails of all its objectives and ends in the disarmament of the vanquished spells complete ruin. This will soon be apparent to everybody, although remnants of the scattered force are still using the old, threatening language. It is a safe prophecy that a stabilization conference [1] will take place in the near future and that all nations will then adopt the automatic Gold Standard—that is to say, will stabilize their price-levels and keep them stable by means of gold and silver, in the manner suggested by the President of the United States. It is possible that, at the Conference, America may agree to return to her old buying-price for gold; that would avoid the necessity of any devaluation on the Continent. It is more likely that new levels will be adopted. Thus, the salvation of the world which might have been accomplished in 1933 at the World Economic Conference, will be

[1] September 20th.—Stabilization is now being discussed hopefully all over the world.

accomplished some two years later. This would happen, even if England was unwilling, because the weight of gold in America and France is too great to be resisted (see Fig. 11).[1] Happily there is reason to believe that the British Government, as well as the Bank of England, is prepared for action.

Nevertheless, it must be recognized that there are persons of authority in this country who are opposed, even yet, to the idea of price stabilization. Pathetically, they cling to the old ideas about international jealousies and exert themselves, in consequence, to exorcize the Nationalist spirit from the European nations. It is time that all such good people should be brought to realize that it was only by means of this Nationalist spirit that the leaders of the European peoples were able to obtain enough money to save their followers from destitution and famine. Small wonder that even the most tearful pleas for its abandonment fell on deaf ears. Indeed, it may almost be said that in these lean and dreadful years, France was as necessary to Germany as was Germany to France. But we need not look across the Channel. Already the expenditure on military aircraft is bringing hope and even comfort to many an honest English home. It will stand for ever as the supreme condemnation of the Debt System that the only idealism of which it took account was that associated with war. There was always, in the last issue, money to buy guns and shells and poison

[1] The sharp rise in English prices which has accompanied the crisis at Geneva is likely to hasten the coming of stabilization.—September 20th, 1935.

gas. In their despair the nations of Europe fanned their hate and put the lives of their boys in pawn that boys and girls might live.

Now, at last, without conferences or pilgrimages, the work upon which so much shoe-leather has been expended in these last days, will be accomplished. For men do not wish to murder one another, but only to live together in peace. As, slowly, it comes to be known that the Monstrous Parasite is dead, and that, in consequence, the means of exchange is no longer a monopoly of greed and callous selfishness, the rumours of war will grow faint across Europe's fair fields. Armies and navies and air forces will be put away, because men will have need no longer to live in frenzy that they and their children may eat bread.

BOOK III

VICTORY

CHAPTER XIII

DOLLAR FOR DOLLAR

THE essential fact of the economic situation, as it exists to-day, is that the Masters of Money have lost control of the established basis of credit, gold, and have failed to compel the world to adopt a new basis over which they might have exercised control.[1] Not one cent of all that mountainous stock of gold, of which Mr. Roosevelt took possession in January 1934, lies within reach of the Money Power. International finance cannot move it, now, out of America. No "corner" now can be made in gold. No movement of the foreign exchanges can suck away the metal. Only a beggarly million or two remains to the moneylenders of all the glittering hoard by which, once, the universe was held in thrall.

As has been seen, there was hope to substitute sterling for gold as the world's money. That hope was based fundamentally on the self-contained character of the British Empire and upon the fact that London is the greatest of all markets for food and raw materials. Men, it was argued, must have sterling in order to enter England's markets and must, therefore, hold

[1] By buying and selling gold in London according to the methods so well understood by them.

their monies related to sterling. But this argument contained a fallacy—namely that men are ready to make any sacrifice of patriotism in order to keep their trade. The events of the spring of 1935 have shown that, on the contrary, when national fervour has been roused, peoples will endure almost any hardship sooner than submit to what looks like foreign dictation. A year ago it was being predicted with the utmost confidence that Germany and Italy must soon change their policies because of the impossibility in existing circumstances of obtaining sterling exchange. Since then both the German and Italian peoples have accepted conscription and rationing rather than abate their independence.[1]

There is, indeed, world-wide revolt against money-lending of so determined a kind that any reversal of the verdict of June 6th, 1935, is impossible. Those who comfort themselves with assurances that statesmen and dictators come and go whereas money is eternal will certainly be disappointed. Even Mr. Roosevelt, as he acknowledged, is only the directing force of an irresistible national spirit. Thus, a second great fact of the present situation is its permanence. The Masters of Money have lost their power; they will not regain it.

On the contrary, the debt structure of every country, lacking, as it must for the future, that international

[1] September 20th, 1935.—This fact ought to be borne in mind when the European dictatorships are being blamed. It is matter of rejoicing that Sir Samuel Hoare took account of it at Geneva in connexion with the Italo-Abyssinian Crisis.

support which was its strength, will gradually crumble away. The process is already in active operation. Because price-levels, having fallen to the lowest depths, are now stable, producers of goods, everywhere, are getting out of debt and these producers have the assurance that new falls in their prices will not occur. They can, therefore, look forward and make plans without anxiety. The mischief of a falling price-level resides in the fact that while prices break debts remain unbroken. The world is now engaged in repudiating debts which, in no circumstances, could have been paid. The slate is being wiped clean and the Masters of Money are helpless to prevent the wiping. Nations are beginning to trade goods for goods, without benefit of international lending.

This is occurring even in England, where the National Government has maintained a balanced budget; it is occurring much more quickly in the United States where the budget has, deliberately, been left unbalanced for a few years in order that it may balance itself finally at a new level. It is occurring, too, in Germany, in France, in Italy and in Japan, all of which countries have large deficits on the national accounts. The American Government is borrowing short-term money at the almost farcical figure of 2*s*. per cent per annum—because the American budget is unbalanced. The British Government is paying about 10*s*. per cent per annum because the British budget balances. Nevertheless, Treasury borrowing grows cheaper in spite of all the "Gentlemen's agreements" and "Bankers' Hold Off" pacts by which it has recently been sought to make the Government pay more for private-signature-money.

It cannot be too clearly understood that an unbalanced budget is tantamount to a creation of money by the Government which does not balance its budget. It is, therefore, a challenge to the claim that only private signatures can be " good money ". If the budget has to be balanced then there is no escape from the horrors of slump and unemployment except surrender to the demands of the Masters of Money. Public works schemes, on a balanced budget, are a farce because what is spent on the new works is taken back at once by taxation. For every man who obtains employment some other man has to be dismissed by an employer who can no longer, on account of the extra taxes, afford to pay his wage. This is the true explanation of the so-called " failure " of public works. What is put into the markets with one hand is taken out with the other, so that nobody is any better off.

In the past, as has already been said, the moment any national budget showed sign of becoming unbalanced the foreign exchanges used to be set by the Masters of Money against the defaulting country from which, immediately, gold flowed out, carrying away with it large masses of signature-money. This caused prices to fall and so produced a crisis. The offending government now submitted and balanced its budget. But control of the foreign exchanges implies the power to buy or sell against all comers—implies, that is to say, control of the basis of credit. A government possessed of a great sum in gold can protect its exchange and counter such attacks as may be made upon it. This is what happened in America after Mr. Roosevelt seized the gold stocks. The dollar exchange could not be "rigged" and, consequently, the President could proceed boldly to the unbalancing of his budget. The patriotic movements engendered and led by Herr Hitler and Signor Mussolini furnish an example of an alternative method of reaching the same object. Fortified by popular support a dictator is able to seize the stocks of foreign exchange and so to compel the banks to lend him money, without promise given that the budget will be balanced at once.

As has already been pointed out, such action could not have taken place had not the control of the basis of credit passed out of private hands. Had the Masters of Money been in control the rebellious government would, immediately, have suffered a catastrophic outflow of gold. If it had tried to replace the vanishing gold-money by money created by itself, its own banks, relying upon the external support of the Masters of Money, would have inflated the home-created money until it became worthless.

There is a close connexion, therefore, between Mr. Roosevelt's seizure of the American gold stock and the unbalanced budgets of Germany and France and Italy. That seizure shook the fabric of international finance so that the pressure which could be brought to bear on any government was fatally weakened. The drain of gold to America, moreover, added weakness to weakness in spite of the additional supplies of the metal which came from India and the South African Mines. At the middle of 1934 the Masters of Money abandoned hope of regaining control of the world's gold stock and, as has been seen, turned desperately to sterling as the only possible alternative to gold. The world was edified by the spectacle of the men who had said there was no money but gold, furiously denouncing that metal and demanding its supercession as the universal money.

It is necessary to repeat these statements because, unless the position of gold is understood, the nature of the victory which has been won cannot be understood. Since gold has not been superceded as the basis of money, he who has control of the preponderating weight of the metal can, if he chooses, impose his will on the world.

In America, the banks have passed already into the power of the Government because none of them dare sell Government bonds, their only important security, nor call up Government loans nor refuse to lend to Government. Banks, after all, have to earn their keep. If the Government of the United States ceased to borrow, there would be no means of lending, seeing that, thanks to the stable price-level and the unbalanced budget, all the best private borrowers are already out of debt. To a member of Congress who asked why the Government should borrow at all when it might create money *de novo* Mr. Marriner Eccles, the Governor of the Federal Reserve System, replied that, whereas it cost 0·012 per cent per annum to keep an issue of " greenbacks " in good order, the Government

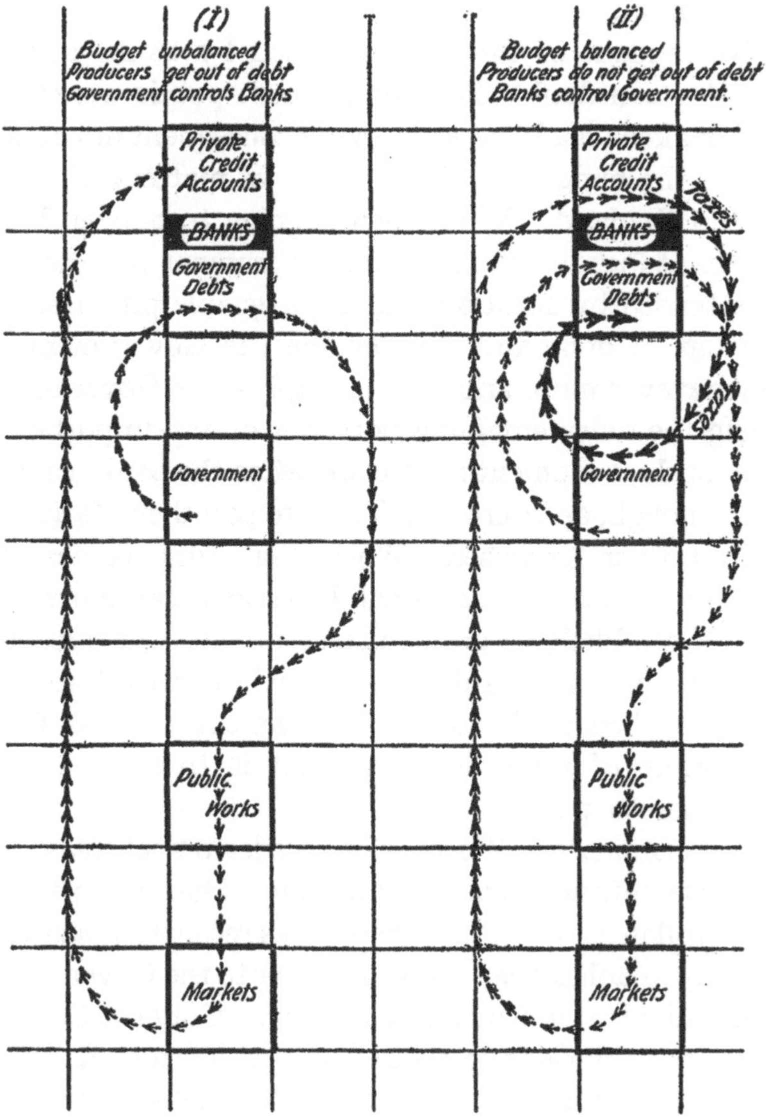

FIG. 12.—PUBLIC WORKS EFFECTIVE AND INEFFECTIVE.

was able to borrow, on short term, at 0·011 per cent per annum.

No student of the reports issued by banks in this country can doubt that, the moment public works are undertaken on a large scale—with consequent unbalancing of the budget—a similar state of matters will prevail in England. What then is going to happen? A glance at Fig. 12 will show how government borrowings, unattended by additional taxation, enable producers to get out of debt and thus enable the Government to borrow ever more and more cheaply—the Government being the only remaining borrower of any importance. Obviously, a moment must come when the banks cannot earn enough, as interest on loans, to pay their staffs and defray their expenses. When that time comes the danger of financial panics will be great because nervous people are likely to grow mistrustful and to make runs on their banks. Banks, sooner or later therefore, will be compelled to go to the Government and ask for a guarantee of their deposits—that is to say of their promises to pay.

Governments will certainly accede to such requests, because refusal would mean ruin. But as certainly they will insist that, when the banks receive a guarantee for, say, a dollar they shall surrender to the Government the equivalent in Government stock. Only the Government has the right to create legal-tender money. The banks will thus be compelled to pay dollar for dollar, pound for pound, for all the legal-tender money supplied to them. National Debts will be wiped out.

CHAPTER XIV

STABILIZATION

At the moment of writing, July 1935, those who realize that the Masters of Money have been beaten are urging an Anglo-American Association for the purpose of securing the peace of the world. Others, less well informed, seem to be anxious to avoid such an association and are making, at present, a great hubbub about the unstable state of American politics, the growing unpopularity of Mr. Roosevelt and the certainty that 1936 will see the end of the New Dealer and his New Deal.

It would be well if these people took the trouble to inform themselves about what has happened, what is now happening and what is bound to happen in the immediate future. Their objection to an Anglo-American Association is, fundamentally, that it means the stabilization of the pound-sterling on a price-index with a gold interpreter, the automatic Gold Standard. They cannot believe that sterling is no longer a weapon capable of effecting the rescue and restoration of the Masters of Money and continue to assure themselves that, if only definite action is avoided, something even at this eleventh hour is bound to turn up whereby a new basis of credit—in the possession of the Masters—will be established.

The reasons for rejecting any such ideas have already been stated. The reasons why the pound must be stabilized in the near future ought to be more clearly understood than appears to be the case. The truth is that the control of the pound-dollar exchange no longer rests exclusively with London. This is obvious when it is recalled that, since the second currency drive, the exchange has moved in the neighbourhood of \$4.94 to £1,[1] whereas the former parity of exchange was \$4.86 to £1. With a substantial "favourable" balance of trade behind it the dollar ought to be more valuable and not less valuable than it was five years ago and would, certainly, be more valuable if steps were not being taken to hold it down.

This cheap dollar gives the American exporter a decided "advantage"—to use the terminology of the Old Economics. In addition, the American exporter is deriving advantage from the size of his home market in which the buying-power of the farmers has been restored, from the stability of the price-level and from the rapidly diminishing burden of bank-debt, both private and public.

Now it is clear that the English exporter cannot face a depreciated dollar, a home market of some 120,000,000 souls, the buying-power of which is rising steadily, and a swiftly falling rate of interest while his own money remains dear as compared with the dollar, while his home market remains deflated by excessive taxation

[1] Even the severe Italo-Abyssinian Crisis has lowered the value of the pound only by 3 cents. (i.e. to \$4·91 to £1) and this in spite of large shipments of gold to America by European hoarders.—September 20th, 1935.

and while interest-rates remain, relatively, very high. Indeed, only one thing could have postponed a decision on this point—namely, a rise, amounting to gross inflation, in the American level of prices.

As has been seen, it was a chief object of the Masters of Money to inflate the American price-level.[1] They were defeated in that enterprise because Mr. Roosevelt had foreseen their design and because fortune favoured him in giving him the Supreme Court's decision about N.R.A. at the very moment when his price-level seemed to be getting out of hand. Since then he has checked " bullish sentiment " by his " tax the rich " bill, by his onslaughts on the utility companies and by his banking control schemes, each of which has had the effect of cowing into submission those who were making ready to act.

In these circumstances the hope of engineering a runaway inflation in America is illusory. Consequently, if the dollar exchange cannot be influenced favourably to sterling, nothing except a sharp deflation of the English price-level can save the English export trade. At a moment when a General Election is approaching such a deflation is not likely to appeal very strongly to the Government, especially since it must inflict as much or more damage on those who supply the home market as it can do good to those who supply foreign markets. The American pressure, moreover, can and will be intensified. The dollar exchange is capable of further falls; the American

[1] In the first instance by a Wall Street boom and a rise of factory prices.

home market is expanding quickly; the burden of debt in America is dwindling away. A policy of deflation in England in such circumstances is a policy of suicide.

Sterling, therefore, like the other currencies of the world, will be stabilized on a price-index and that price-index with suitable emendations will necessarily be adopted by every country in the world, seeing that no country will be able to refuse to adopt it. It is obvious that such a prospect will occasion, very soon, outbursts from persons who suppose that England's place in the world was bestowed upon her by money-lenders and that, without these moneylenders and their offices, she is doomed to lose her trade, her strength and finally her Empire.

Such misguided folk may be invited, for their comfort, to ask themselves how England would have fared had Wall Street become the moneylending centre of the world. The writer was told, early in 1931, by a distinguished American banker, that:

"We take the view that you people are on the toboggan. You've had your day; our time has come."

What was meant was that, in future, private-signature-money in large quantities would be obtainable only in New York. Had that occurred, as has already been said, nothing but a miracle could have saved the British Empire.

A further means of solace is to be found in the question how a system which works only by beating down wages in every country against wages in every other country can be helpful to trade, that is to say, the buying of goods. Wages are buying-power. It is obvious that the Debt System of money has destroyed a hundred times more trade than it has ever promoted, seeing that low wages represent a small capacity to buy and so to absorb goods.

Nor is there a pennyworth of substance in the assertion that " as England lives by her export Trade ", she will cease to live unless she imports huge quantities of foreign stocks and bonds—that is to say, of foreign paper—in exchange for her products. England does not live by paper; nevertheless, during the latter quarter of the Nineteenth Century, she received some £7,000,000,000 worth of that commodity over and above the actual goods which came to her harbours. Some £3,000,000,000 of the paper is now worth nothing. Consequently, England in five-and-twenty years or so gave away free gratis and for nothing £3,000,000,000 of real wealth. Is it seriously contended that a country which can distribute largesse on this scale, after it has imported the food it is able to consume, is going to starve because it will not be required, any longer, to make such handsome gifts—not indeed to foreign peoples but to its own and foreign moneylenders? As well suggest that a plague of locusts enriches the farmer across whose fields it passes.

Mr. Roosevelt's stabilization proposal puts no country " on the toboggan ". It ties the economy of no foreign land to irresponsible persons in some distant capital city. It secures no territorial aggrandizement, no right to exercise scrutiny or force. It imposes no deflation of any kind on any country or on any individual. All it does—but it does this effectively—is to deliver the world from the slavery of debt.

The policy of the British Government, as enunciated first at Ottawa and then at the World Economic Conference, bears a striking resemblance to Mr. Roosevelt's policy. At Ottawa it was declared unanimously:

> It is also, in the view of the Conference, of the utmost importance to the future working of any international standard that international co-operation should be secured and maintained with a view to avoiding so far as may be found practicable, wide fluctuations in the purchasing-power of the standard of value. [1]

And that view was re-affirmed in the "Imperial Declaration" made in London at the meeting of the Colonial premiers in 1933. In these circumstances the British Government should have no difficulty in coming to an agreement with Mr. Roosevelt and so laying the foundations of a union of the English-speaking peoples to preserve peace. Such a union would make war almost as archaic as moneylending is likely to become.

Imperial Economic Conference, 1932, p. 24.

CHAPTER XV

PRICE AND VALUE

It is important that there should be a clear understanding of what is meant by the term " price-level " because great confusion is apt to arise when this term is mentioned. A price-level is not the price of any given substance or commodity—wheat, for example. Rather it is an average of the prices of a large number of substances, though the word average is not strictly accurate because commodities are " weighted " (or handicapped like golfers) when the average is made up. Pepper, for instance, would not rank equally with beef in a well-made index. When the weighted average has been arrived at it is rendered as a percentage of the weighted average on some chosen day or year which, in consequence, is called 100. The price-level consists of the percentage of the chosen level which obtained on any other day. Thus, one might say that the price-level in 1913 was below the 1926 level whereas the level in 1919 was above it.

The choice of the day or year or period of years which is to be called 100 is a purely arbitrary matter. Any time is as good as any other time. Nor is the weighting of the average so important as some economists seem to believe. Ordinary averages give results which do not differ very greatly from those obtained by weighting. The important thing in an index is the number of commodities which it contains. The United States Bureau of Labour Index is based on 784 commodities, that of the British Board of Trade on 200 commodities.

An index is procured daily from the prices actually obtained in the markets. Consequently, it affords a clear picture of the upward or downward trend of *all* prices together—that is to say of the amount of buying-power in the markets. If all prices are tending to rise there is too much buying-power in the markets; if all prices are tending to fall there is too little. In the former case the necessary corrective will be the removal of surplus money; in the latter case the supply of additional money.

But the money must leave the markets or go into the markets as the case may be. The mere addition of money to the country's total stock can achieve nothing in the way of price raising unless the new money *comes onto the counter*. And it by no means follows that this will happen. If money comes to the pockets of rich men it is likely to be saved or invested, possibly in foreign countries. Such saving or foreign lending need not mean any additional buying in *this* country. Money on the contrary which is given to the poor goes to market at once and so influences prices.

The business of a monetary commission under the new stabilization system will be to keep the price index at 100. The Commission will, therefore, be concerned to employ methods of correction which can be trusted to act immediately. As has already been seen, the automatic Gold Standard is such a method. The automatic Gold Standard keeps the price index of any given country steady by bringing buyers to or driving buyers away from the market of that country. The system possesses the great advantage that it acts itself, mechanically, and with a minimum of delay. The use of silver in addition to gold prevents any tampering with this automatic action.

If, for example, a great mass of goods of all kinds reaches the American market so that the price-level falls, then buyers from England and elsewhere will enter that market and raise prices by bidding for the goods with gold. This gold will be made the basis of an output of dollars. Should a case arise, however, in which all countries participated equally in the flood of new goods, the international standard would not effect the necessary correction because prices would fall equally everywhere. Correction in this instance could be effected by an international agreement to raise the price of gold. As the metal will never again be allowed to remain anywhere in private hands, that would be a very simple operation.

With the purely technical means employed to give effect to the policy of stable prices it is unnecessary to concern oneself. The public will possess, at all times, in the published figures, an accurate measure of the success which is attending the efforts of its servants. Only the Masters of Money have ever cast a doubt on the possibility of maintaining the index figure at 100 from month to month and year to year, and their criticisms have lost all substance since Sweden established her index. Their utmost endeavours, which, as has been seen, have embraced every country on earth, have failed to make any impression on the stability of American prices so that it can now be said with assurance that, if a price-level is not being maintained, such failure is due to the incompetence of the currency authorities. Every citizen will, in the days to come, see printed in his newspaper each week the index-number for the week before. He will, therefore, know what the price-level is doing and, consequently, what is happening to the value of his money. Public opinion will thus supply the driving-force necessary to secure competence in public officials.

A properly managed price index is, indeed, the charter of democracy in any real meaning of that word. For not only does it guarantee the buying-power of money, that is to say the worth of money, but also the freedom of the holder of money to buy what he wants. Reference has already been made to the price pattern of a country, that is to say to the relationships existing, between groups of prices, for example between farm prices and factory prices. It must now be insisted that, when the price-level is held stable, the price pattern will represent truly the will of the people, always provided that interferences with the pattern by foreign countries can be prevented. The ruin of the American price pattern in 1929 was brought about while the price-level was stable; it was not brought about by any action of the American people but by the fact that America was dependent upon foreign markets for the disposal of her cotton crop. The Masters of Money, by means which have already been described, destroyed the buying-power of Europe and thus broke the American price pattern. That can never happen again. In any case, thanks to Mr. Roosevelt, the United States is now in a position to protect its markets against foreign pressure. When price-levels, therefore, are stabilized, price patterns will everywhere reflect the needs and desires of men and women.

This is obvious when it is recalled that men spend their incomes, first and foremost, on food and clothing. Farm prices bear a natural, inevitable and, to a certain extent, invariable relationship to all other prices; and consequently a normal pattern shows them, always in balance with all other prices. If they are out of balance the reason can only be artificial manipulation. (*World-wide* famine or bumper crops *in every land* might effect some maladjustment but such things do not happen.) To accept any other explanation would be to suppose that people had ceased to eat or had decided to abandon the wearing of clothes.

It follows that all efforts to "plan" economy, in the sense of interfering with production, are futile when a stable level of prices has been attained. Such efforts, happily, in such circumstances, cannot possibly succeed because, as has been said, a stable price-level is a see-saw. If one end of the see-saw is raised the other end must fall. The planners can, for example, reduce the costs of making say copper wire by a process of "rationalization" involving the reduction of wages or the dismissal of workpeople. But since both reduction of wages and the dismissal of workpeople involve a loss of buying-power in markets, and since this buying-power will be replaced at once (by increased unemployment insurance and other means), it will soon be necessary for the rationalizing firm to pay the employees who remain on its books larger wages. In consequence, no additional profits will be earned. The same argument applies to combines and trusts existing for the purpose of raising the prices of goods. As the price of, say, pork goes up the prices of beef and mutton and poultry will fall because pork-buyers will have less money to spend on them. In consequence, people will " change over " from pork to beef and the pork-combine will lose its profit.

Thus, it can be stated, generally, that no monopoly and no process of rationalization involving the cutting of wages can possibly succeed under a stable price-level system. What can occur under the system, however, is a cheapening of goods brought about by improved technical method and such cheapening will, of course, raise the prices of other goods. That will enable producers in other fields to spend money on new machinery and better methods and so, in their turn, to cheapen production. Thus the whole benefit of technical knowledge will be passed on to the public by stages until a point has been reached where all the needs of the population are being satisfied. Beyond this point surplus goods will be exchanged for the surplus goods of other countries until no country cares to absorb any more goods of any kind.

As has been seen, the guiding-force in this development will be money—the will of the people expressed through an " economic voting system " which permits every kind of choice and which puts no fetters upon any chooser. Goods which lose their popularity will soon disappear from markets ; nor can there be any bolstering up of markets for the sake of the " capital " invested in them. Every investor must take the risk that his particular kind of service to the public may not please the public.

The difference between this system and the system now in operation is the difference between service and compulsion. The existing system is founded not upon price but upon what is called " value "—namely an estimate or forecast of price. A price is what the public has actually paid for an article ; a " value " is what the public is expected to pay. Expectation, as things stand, can be helped towards realization by such devices as a " Futures " Market in which prices are arranged months and even years ahead of sales. Thus there are " futures " for wheat, cotton, sugar, rubber, silver and indeed all commodities. The wheat crop has changed hands again and again before it is sown and the price which it actually fetches is some kind of compromise between Nature and the speculators.

Value has become, in this way, not a measure of worth to the community but a means of forcing the community to pay speculators' prices. The speculator justifies himself by declaring that he " makes a market " ; but this is precisely what he ought not to do. It is the public which ought to make the market.

" Futures " offer an illustration of the economic fallacy

that value is measured by the amount spent in producing the goods without relation to their usefulness. This is the fallacy on which the Marxian philosophy is based. According to this philosophy an Atlantic liner which had been built on the top of Ben Nevis ought to be worth the cost of building it. The philosophy is essentially brutal because it carries invariably the threat that "if the public is not prepared to buy at our price the public must be compelled to do so". Compulsion in Russia is by bayonet and bomb; elsewhere systems of "options" and "futures" perform the same office. "Positions" are "built up" by "operators" on the commodity exchanges—usually with the help of moneylenders—and goods are disposed of in such a way as to defeat the law of supply and demand.

The moment the level of prices has been stabilized, this edifice of coercion will fall because it will be wholly impossible to fix or rig or anticipate any price. As has been seen, the see-saw action of the fixed level will punish instantly any attempt to raise prices and will thus make all prices subject to the popular will.

This truth is being illustrated at the moment of writing (July 1935) by the conditions in the wheat markets of the world. It was an integral part of the plan of the Masters of Money, as has already been pointed out, to cause an industrial boom in the United States as the first step in the production of an inflationary boom. In consequence, heavy "bull positions" were "built up" in wheat and other commodities. The positions depended for their safety on the belief that the Canadian Government would not dispose of its surplus stock of some 230,000,000 bushels except at a comparatively high price.

Unhappily for the speculators the Canadian Government seems to be anxious to adopt the principles that were laid down at Ottawa and is ready in consequence to get rid of a surplus which, during years, has been a curse to the Prairie Provinces so that, in the new wheat year (July 1, 1935, to June 30, 1936) a stabilized price-level may be instituted and the crop consumed. On July 6th, in consequence, " the bottom fell out of the wheat market ". The Canadian wheat will now be sold to a world which has need of it. When the new harvest begins to appear production and consumption will be about equal and the way will be open for an expansion of both to any extent.[1]

[1] September 20th.—Since this was written Nature has taken a hand and so greatly reduced the stocks of wheat that no surplus any longer exists.

CHAPTER XVI

THE FUTURE OF MARKETS

THE stabilization of price-levels throughout the world will effect, therefore, release of the world, more or less rapidly, from all forms of moneylending and from all forms of "futures" trading. The tolls payable formerly for these activities will be saved and the prices of goods will fall to levels which will greatly astonish both producers and consumers. Producers will still obtain their former profits and consumers will be able to add all kinds of new luxuries to their way of living.

But this fall of prices as a consequence of the disappearance of moneylending must be distinguished clearly from a fall in the price-level. That will be maintained at 100 no matter how greatly individual prices are falling. Consequently, articles the prices of which were less influenced by "futures" trading or rates of interest will find a growing market (people will have more money to spend on them) and will rise in price. An oyster bed may be taken as an example. The rise in price, as has been suggested, will cause an expansion of production and soon another delicacy will become widely available.

The structure of all markets will now undergo important change. Speculation will gradually disappear and will take with it most of the " Exchanges ". Men possessed of good businesses will possess also the assurance that their businesses are not going to be ruined by sudden falls in price and will, consequently, hand them on to their sons. There will be small temptation to " float " such concerns as companies and the Stock Market, in consequence, will dwindle to very small proportions—for no bonds or debentures or other forms of debt will any longer be on sale, all having been paid off. Further, insurance will begin to look like an expensive luxury when there is plenty of money available to every producer and householder to meet the emergencies of fire or theft. Better buildings will be the way out of the fire danger; a higher standard of living will cure many of the social evils—all those associated with poverty. Thus it is improbable that any kind of insurance will flourish in the civilization that is now about to be built up.

Nor is this remarkable when it is recalled that insurance is, essentially, a form of moneylending. Insurance offices like Building Societies prosper by obtaining money at low rates and lending it at higher rates, and it matters nothing whether such money is called " premium " or " instalment ". It is true that the customer of the Insurance Company or Building Society obtains something for his money—namely security or shelter; but that ought not to obscure the fact that he is borrowing at substantial rates of interest. The customer of the Insurance Company is borrowing a sum of money for future delivery. Meanwhile, he is paying back capital and interest in a series of instalments, so arranged as to cover the possibility that the borrowed money may have to be delivered sooner than was expected. On an average the Insurance Company gets back what has been borrowed, along with a high rate of interest, before the policy becomes due for payment. In other words the customer has saved a certain sum of money and has paid the Insurance Company interest upon his savings. The moment the customer has enough money of his own to cover the risks of life and work he will naturally invest his savings in some business and so take the profit for himself instead of giving it to the Insurance Company. He will no longer insure.

In the case of the Building Society borrowing takes place for immediate delivery and capital and interest are repaid in process of years. The customer does not become the owner of the house until the final instalment has been paid and is therefore merely a tenant who is paying a high rent in addition to all costs of upkeep and repair and all owner's costs. A man who can afford to do otherwise, does not enter into contracts of this kind. Building Societies, therefore, will gradually cease to exist.

But these two examples by no means exhaust the forms of moneylending which surround all our lives. Rent is moneylending; so also are wages.

Those who find such statements difficult may be invited to consider in what, exactly, moneylending or usury consists. What is the quality which is common to a bank overdraft, an insurance policy, a Building

Society contract, a tenancy and a salary or wage? The answer is the immunity of the lender from the ordinary risks and dangers of life upon this earth. The banker, when he made his loan, took security of a value not less than double the value of his loan. He is "covered" as to principal and interest in any event. That is to say, he has secured a certain income no matter what may happen to his customer. And all he lent was his signature. The Insurance Company, as has been seen, lent nothing except a promise to pay in certain eventualities. It, too, has received a certain income no matter what may happen to the mass of its customers. The Building Society lent the use of a house for a fixed rate of interest plus the upkeep of the house and the payment of all the burdens on the house. It still possesses its capital. It has secured a certain income no matter what may happen to the mass of its customers.

This is the position, also, of the landlord who, however, gets less, as a rule, than the Building Society. It is, too, in a way the position of the person receiving a fixed salary or wage because he has to be paid no matter what may happen to his employer's business.

In each case the penalty for default is the same. If the borrower fails to repay, his goods are seized. Failure to keep up the payment of premiums or of instalments results in loss of monies already paid or in eviction from the house. Employees, if their master cannot pay their wages, can seize his goods. The unhappy victim is always liable to be turned out on the road without food or shelter, in other words, to be condemned to death. However disguised, money-lending is a threat system, the basis of which is legalized murder. What is really hired out is neither money nor houses nor labour, but Time. Payment is made per cent per annum. If there is no payment then time ceases so far as the defaulter is concerned.

It is not suggested, of course, that any such extreme effects have attended the majority of the operations of usurers, and it is obvious that, as things have been, a fixed wage was the only protection the wage-earners possessed. What is under discussion is a principle against which, instinctively, human nature recoils. Who has not heard an employer, faced with ruin himself, speaking bitterly about his men "and their snug wages that have to be paid whether or no"? Who has not in prosperous times heard employees talking about "the boss's huge earnings of which we get not a penny piece"? Both sides feel the same sense of injustice. And both are right. There is no "whether or not" in Nature.

An example of what is meant has been furnished by the tithe. While tithes were paid in kind, they were paid gladly to God's good man. Now that they are paid in money, farmers, ruined by falling prices, curse the clergy and have in one instance, at least, burned the Archbishop of Canterbury in effigy. And why? Because a tithe which has to be paid in money may be a demand that a man shall give what he does not possess.

And here we come to the sap and marrow of usury and fixed payments in general. *They are magic.*

There never have been such things and there never can be such things. No man has ever eaten bread from a blighted field, nor snatched apples from a bare tree, nor taken lobsters from an empty pot, nor drunk water from a dry well. There is no such thing as a riskless life and neither life itself nor possessions can be insured in a world " where moth and rust do corrupt and where thieves break through and steal ". The moneylender with his fixed interest does not, thereby, abolish the laws of God, though he may seem to have done so. He does not expel or exorcize risk from the world. What he really does is to load a part of his personal risk on to the shoulders of his customer. His customer's trees may not bear fruit; but if they don't he will seize them all and sell them and buy fruit for himself. And he will believe that, by so doing, he has vindicated the law of usury—namely that money breeds. If the ewes of the sheep farmer do not give birth to lambs, why then one can eat the ewes. If the employer has had his crops destroyed by locusts, does not the man himself remain to be devoured?

The usurer is an illusionist, a wizard, a conjurer who can apparently bring rabbits out of empty hats. But the rabbits have to be supplied by somebody. Nature knows nothing of fixed payments. Sometimes she is generous; sometimes a miser. At best men can treasure her gifts from one season to another. A system based on a contrary view is not only unscientific but also, fundamentally, absurd. Fundamentally it represents the oldest of all the illusions—namely that the shadow is the substance, the symbol the thing symbolized. When a moneylender makes a loan to a farmer at interest he is, in sober fact, pretending to determine in advance how many lambs the man's ewes will produce several years ahead, how many bushels shall be won from his fields, and what weight of fruit his orchards are going to bestow. The accountancy of production has been transformed into the fecundity of figures, and we are back to the savage who will not allow anyone to paint his portrait because, if that were done, he might be murdered by the simple process of stabbing the canvas with a penknife.

The principle of the fixed price-level destroys instantly the illusion of the symbol, money, by enabling all men to get out of debt. Men who are out of debt treat money as the receipt for goods or services delivered and, therefore, as an order to obtain goods and services. They do not need to pay it away in order to buy time—the right to live. Consequently, they are in small danger of confusing it with wealth or of looking upon it as the only wealth, the attitude of the overwhelming majority of persons at the present day.

The stable level of prices will destroy the money illusion and the money magic; and with these wizardries will pass the other wizardries that have attended them, economic, political and religious. Men will cease to hire and will begin to buy. They will cease to hoard and will begin to use. They will cease to worship idols and will begin to enjoy God.

And poverty will fly away. It is not generally known that, in the Thirteenth Century, Englishmen and all Europeans had some 150 holidays every year (100 holy days of obligation and 52 Sundays); that they possessed a higher standard of nutrition than that enjoyed at the present day; that they were so rich that every village, almost, could build a noble cathedral. These people had only their muscles and the muscles of horses and oxen, in addition to a few windmills and waterwheels, as their sources of power. The present world is equipped with a power plant some millions of times more effective. But holidays have nearly vanished and public works can scarcely be undertaken at all.

The people of the Thirteenth Century had stable prices and moneylending was forbidden among them. When the people of the Twentieth Century have the same blessings they will make a garden of their world. For the money will come with the goods so that the goods may be used. It will come as pensions, as endowments of age, of infirmity and of weakness. It will come, later, as a portion of citizenship. Indeed the only fear is that the stream of goods even then may outrun the stream of money. Taxation in all its forms will dwindle to vanishing-point. And no man, in that world of abundance, will save a farthing.

CHAPTER XVII

THE EXCELLENCE OF PROFIT

MEN who possess enough money to start in business for themselves do not, as a rule, seek employment as wage-earners. As money becomes more widely distributed, therefore, wages will inevitably rise. This rise will enable more wage-earners to go into business for themselves. In the end wages will disappear and be replaced by partnerships of one kind or another.

At first this gradual elimination of the human element from industry will produce an increase in the use of machines, and mass-production; goods will become more and more machine-made goods in the strictest sense of that term. But, since this process will be accompanied by the replacement of wages by pensions and dividends (so that the price-level may be maintained) a movement in a different direction will gradually begin to show itself. Men do not hate work; on the contrary, every healthy man if left to himself will, sooner or later, find something to do—something to make. And this work, which he has chosen, will give him joy and recreation as well as occupation. If its products are welcomed by his neighbours it will afford him, in addition, a most lively satisfaction. Thus the products of craftsmanship are likely to appear once more upon markets.

It is matter of observation that people who can afford to buy specially produced goods seldom buy mass-production goods. Craftsmanship will come, therefore, at the moment when the virtue of craftsmanship is beginning to make a new appeal to men because men possess the means of acquiring it. The machine will now fall to second place and a gradual selection be made between goods which, as all are agreed, can best be made by machines and goods which it is better to make by hand. Here, as everywhere, demand will rule and direct supply. The machines, acting by themselves, will be under the control of Master Craftsmen—highly skilled engineers and their apprentices. The machines will do the dirty work. They will supply the basis of craftsmanship.

Thus science will be brought to the service of men not as universal provider but as universal helper.

It will now be decided, not by public debate or Act of Parliament but by the open ballot of the markets, what standard of living men desire to possess. It may be, for example, that the population as a whole is content with what it already has. In that event the demand for goods will not increase with increased buying-power and gradually the supply of goods will shrink. This will be a vote for leisure and against luxury. But it will be open to any citizen to work as hard as he chooses and so, by a surrender of leisure, to obtain more luxury than his fellows. The population, again, may display a great desire for goods and so quickly empty the markets. The markets will soon be filled again with new goods and the standard of living will rise. But, again, it will be open to any citizen to live frugally and so obtain leisure.

The probability is that the world will continue to follow its present bent of demanding a rising standard of living. We may look, therefore, for the complete transformation of the apparatus of life—houses, roads, production, farming, manufacture, amusement—with, on one side, an ever-increasing mechanization and on the other an ever-increasing demand for beautiful and highly differentiated products. Guilds will be resurrected and reformed, artisans, in Napoleon's phrase, will become artists. That excellent criticism which has its foundations in the spirits, as opposed to the wits, of men will inform and instruct the makers of all things.

And the motive ? Profit tempered by competition. To say that it is base or selfish to wish to earn a profit is to say that when a farmer sows seed he ought to banish from his mind all thought of harvest. Men sow to reap—and to reap as much more than they have sown as it may be possible to obtain. Men buy raw materials in order to make of them things of as great worth as it may be possible to make. Craftsmanship is profit-making ; so is art ; so is poetry. But the profit lies within the goods themselves and not outside of them in ledgers.

The gardener, for example, who can grow more

beautiful roses than his fellows is employing earth and labour and material to greater profit than his fellows. That greater profit can, and should, be recorded in ledgers because it is recorded already in roses and will be recorded in the joy of those to whom the roses are sold. Everyone will share the profit—even posterity to whom the Master's secrets will be handed down, and rivals who will learn to what inferior use they have put their materials.

It may be said, indeed, that the only way in which a man can love his neighbours is to earn profit in making goods for them. And the greater the profit the more excellent the love. True craftsmanship glows with love; "a thing of beauty is a joy for ever". Competition is of the essence of craftsmanship seeing that competition is a rivalry in service and therefore a criticism of those who serve. Here, again, it is the shadow which has darkened judgment. A money-profit ought to be nothing but the record of a real profit. Instead it has become the real profit so that the production of evil and shoddy goods is called "profitable" in defiance of the evidence of eyes and fingers. Such money-profits cannot be obtained when buyers are well supplied with money, because people buy inferior goods only when they are compelled by poverty to do so. In the future profit and money-profit, like wealth and money-wealth, will cease to be names with different applications. The whole of the prejudice against "the profit motive" will then disappear, and the absurd notion that shoddy produced by a government or a borough council is somehow preferable to shoddy produced by an individual will cease to bemuse honest minds.

Shoddy will disappear because there will be no market for shoddy and no money-profit to be made out of it. Skilled production will replace shoddy because there will be a market for skilled production. Thus profit will, naturally and properly, be reflected in money-profit and not, as at present, money-profit in profit. Just as poverty keeps men in debt and induces them to suppose that the means of paying debt is wealth, so also poverty forces them to make and sell rubbish goods and induces them to believe that, if they can obtain more money for these goods than was expended in production, they are "making" profits.

Socialists, and especially guild socialists, have some inkling of this truth. But few, if any of them, seem to have been able to look beyond the money illusion. Instead therefore of addressing themselves to the reform of the monetary system they continue to waste their own and other people's time by attacking the object they desire to attain—namely, a more excellent craftsmanship, profit. In the same way they are concerned to raise wages instead of to abolish them, and to divide "wealth" instead of to increase it. When a Socialist speaks of wealth he always means money and usually shows, in addition, that he supposes money to be a rare and precious commodity, the amount of which can scarcely be increased. This is the doctrine of the Masters of Money.

Owing to incapacity to differentiate between wealth and money, that is between things and figures, socialists soon convince themselves that one man is rich because another man is poor (which again is the view of the Masters of Money) and strive, therefore, by Trades Unions and other means to obtain larger shares of money for their protégés instead of busying themselves to create larger quantities of goods and to secure that money shall be available to enable the goods to be consumed. The only argument in favour of taxing the rich to give money to the poor is that poor men spend whereas rich men often hoard, and that, in consequence, such taxation amounts to a campaign against hoarding and in favour of spending. But why all the bother when, by the simple device of a fixed price-level, bother can be avoided? The only substantial title to any possession is that bestowed by the consumption of one's neighbours. If the owner of a boot factory cannot sell his boots he loses boots and factory immediately. The truth is that the rich are poorer than they need be because the poor are poor. Wealth, in other words, which cannot be used, is not wealth but waste. Socializing waste does not turn it into wealth, nor is waste changed in quality by changing its ownership. Socialism is, thus, a mere crying in the wilderness. Now that the Masters of Money have been defeated, the rigid limits set upon the issue of the means of exchange will disappear, carrying with them to Limbo all the fallacies and absurdities that they have engendered. Socialists will then begin to concern themselves with wealth and profit because waste will exist no longer to whet their acquisitiveness.

Nor are they likely, in these days, to wish to "take

over the means of production and distribution", seeing that the public will already be in control of both by virtue of its power to buy all the goods and services on the market. It must be said for the Masters of Money that they never embarked on the enterprise of conducting personally the businesses and factories which fell into their hands, but invariably left such conduct to persons quallified by knowledge and experience. Socialists possess, apparently, none of this wisdom. They are like shepherds who wish to grow wool on their own backs so that they may experience an added joy of ownership.

Socialism is now doomed, therefore, and will soon disappear as superfluous and absurd. With it will go Big Labour and all the Trades Unions, which depend on the wage system and on the system of Debt Money with its limitations and restrictions. In place of the Trades Unions will come again the Guilds with their real-profit motive and their good competition. For Trades Unions are, essentially, a means of protecting producers against consumers, whereas Guilds exist to safeguard the highest interests of both. The Trades Unions movement was born out of the Debt System, as a means of rescuing the weak from the horrors of utter destitution and degradation. It deserves the very best which any man can say of it or think of it. But its abundant justification lay outside of itself in the assaults upon decency and mercy of the Great Enemy. Now that the Great Enemy has been destroyed, the ramparts which courage and faith built against him must inevitably crumble to ruin.

Enterprise, in short, will be private and not public, except in a few instances. And businesses will tend to become smaller in size and not bigger. Big Business is a creation of the Masters of Money. Like Big Labour it constituted, to some extent, a reaction against the Money Power. A big business could "command" capital whereas a small business had to beg for it, and the rates of interest usually reflected this difference, with disastrous consequences for the small business. Again, a big business could command cheap raw materials by using the resources of the Money Market —sometimes by threatening not to use them. If Big Business created a monopoly that monopoly was not broken by the fall of the prices of other goods, because the Masters of Money were always ready to oblige with a modest degree of inflation where very large amounts of capital were at stake.

But to-morrow the small man will labour no longer under the handicaps which the big man used to impose on him. Electrical power will be available to all, big and small, at the same rates—much lower rates than any private firm would require to pay if it installed its own plant. Big and small will trade, equally, on money owned by them and owing to nobody. Big and Small will alike be powerless to influence in any way the general level of prices. In consequence, competition will be for real profit —the excellence of goods. And here the small man has the advantage of the big one. He is giving personal attention to his organization and to those who are co-operating with him; he is personally known to his customers. His products are likely to be better than those of the great factory or machine-shop. His products will carry him to victory.

CHAPTER XVIII

PLAIN MAN'S CHARTER

How will all this affect the lives of men and women? Most men and women grow up, live their lives and die without ever learning how a sixpence goes into circulation. They know, literally, nothing about money except the earning and spending of it. A vague idea, perhaps, exists in their minds that money was created when the world was created.

Nevertheless, every man and every woman has lived his or her life until now under the direct compulsion of the monetary system. This has been said already; it must be repeated, because there are no exceptions to the rule. Upon each of us has been laid the iron necessity of obtaining a certain quantity of money in order to live, or if not to live, at least to pay rates and other fixed outgoings. Money meant private-signature-money; we could obtain it only from the Masters whose signatures alone were valid. We had, therefore, so to rule our lives that this necessary supply, this indispensable supply, reached us in due season. In consequence, every life has been lived under the shadow of an anxiety from which there was no escape. Shall we be able to pay our way? Shall we obtain the money necessary to keep us out of trouble? No matter how rich a man might be there was always the chance that he might lose his money, and the rich, therefore, experienced the same anxiety as the poor, perhaps even a more acute anxiety. Balzac did not exaggerate when he said that the most terrible misfortune which could befall any man was the loss of his money. To-day we stand on the brink of a world in which nobody will experience anxiety about money.

We possess the goods, and the means of making the goods, which we require. We possess, at the same time, armies of reserve workers, the unemployed, who can, if necessary, be called upon to make more goods, and huge idle power plants upon which our reserve armies can work. We are immensely rich, enormously and incredibly rich, richer than men have ever been or have ever dreamed of becoming since the world began. And from now onwards our ledgers are to record facts and not the fancies of Money Masters. This great wealth will appear, for the first time, in humanity's account books so that humanity may make use of it. In short, it will find its true reflection in the money-mirror.

When the goods come to market the money will come with them. In a very short space of time, therefore, the whole population, the whole body of consumers, will be supplied with orders to deliver these abundant goods, that is to say with money. There need be no delay because money costs nothing. (It takes time and trouble to make a brick, a cigarette, a sheet of paper; but any fool can make money.) In a very short space of time, therefore, the Great Fear will be lifted from men's lives.

A somewhat similar fear existed at one time in the form of epidemic disease. The Black Death killed, roughly, about half the population of Europe. It left behind it a deep-seated uneasiness, amounting to panic, which for centuries was a dominating force in the thoughts of men. This pneumonic plague came again and again, so also did bubonic plague, and cholera. Typhoid fever was never absent. Typhus fever attended every war. "A mother's son was never her own till he had had the smallpox."

Then came Jenner and Pasteur and Lister and the fear of pestilence was broken. A shadow was removed from men's minds. There was a new sense of security and a new hope of active and healthy life. The expectation of life increased by some twenty years. Fear was overcome. Disease, indeed, possessed only one remaining rampart—namely, poverty.

Poverty is fallen. Once again a shadow of fear is passing from human life. Once again we shall see the effect in every home and upon every individual. Under the influence of fear men are restless, bitter, cruel, inclined to attack and hurt one another. When fear goes, rest and judgment take its place. There is no longer the fervent demand for excitement wherewith to overcome fear nor the impulse to inflict fear on others so that we may charm it away from ourselves.

The world will become more genial, more kindly, calmer, happier, more tranquil. Every person in the world will be a better person because a less fearful person. Mental health will improve and, with it, bodily health. The diseases which have their origin in anxiety and nervous strain—all of which diseases have been increasing greatly—will begin to diminish. Even such mundane functions as digestion will improve.

And there will be better food to digest, a more balanced diet for everyone. This again will help to abolish tuberculosis in all its protean forms. It was observed, during the War, that, when the German Army entered Warsaw and commandeered all the fats in the city to make nitro-glycerine, the incidence of tuberculosis rose at once to the proportions of an acute epidemic. The fat-containing foods are the costly foods and the world as a whole is still suffering from fat-starvation. It follows that, as fats and other expensive foods become freely available, resistance to tuberculosis will enormously increase. Better food and better digestion will give mankind, very quickly, a new standard of health. And to these must be added better exercise. Forty years ago about one-quarter of every doctor's time was spent in treating anæmia, especially the anæmia of young women. Doctors to-day seldom see a case of anæmia because young women have begun to lead more active lives. That rising standard of English " costs " which so horrified the Masters of Money that they resolved to transport the financial centre from London to New York, rescued thousands of English girls, even in the dark days from 1900 to 1914, from debility and weakness. To-morrow there will be playing-fields for every boy and every girl, where fit, well-fed and cheerful young bodies will learn to resist disease and to achieve a glorious health so that they may spend it in making the things and doing the things which their hearts desire to make and do.

Such labour for good profit will be every man's inheritance. In such labour every man will lose himself, as artists and poets and mystics lose themselves, dying to be born again. That is a process attended by great joy so that men who undergo it sing and shout at their work. Once upon a time Europe was full of the song of happy workers and the things that they made remain still, after centuries, to rejoice men's hearts, the great cathedrals, the great secular buildings, the heritage of art and craft, of music and of literature.

Under the Debt System wages were another name for costs, and costs had to be kept down to the lowest possible level in order that the export trade might flourish, in order, that is to say, that as many buyers as possible from foreign markets might be attracted to the home market. The home market, in other words, was kept empty of buying-power so that buying-power might come to it from abroad. But the foreign money which, thus, flowed into the home market was not allowed, as has been seen, to influence home prices as it would, normally, have done. On the contrary it was lent abroad at once and immediately, therefore, left the country again.

In effect, therefore, the foreign buyers brought with them nothing but certificates of debt for the Masters of Money who became possessed of the whole wealth of the world. The restraint upon trade was necessarily terrific because every country was playing the same game. No home market possessed buying-power above the barest necessity of its workers and, consequently, every country was engaged in trying to force goods into the markets of every other country while these markets—one and all—remained empty of buying-power. The cheapest market was necessarily the winner in this race and, consequently, the lower wages could be reduced, or beaten down, the better. White men were in fierce and violent competition with black men and yellow men who could keep body and soul together with less food and less raiment.

It was really a race for private-signature-money. Everybody knew what happened to the losers: they were left with their goods on their hands because nobody at home had any money to buy anything except in the *cheapest* market. That meant imports without exports, buying without selling, (most sane men like to get things on these lines) and, at the end of the journey, no money. And that meant an unbalanced budget, ruined trade and massive unemployment. Which, again, meant a " flight " of money to happier hunting-grounds.

Every government shuddered at the thought of such a state of affairs. No government so much as dreamed of trying to escape by producing its own money because on every occasion in the past on which that method had been tried, the new money had been smashed amid riots and bloodshed. There was no escape. Costs had to be kept down. Wages had to be held at the very lowest possible level at which police forces and even " the military " could hold them.

In consequence, every social reformer became a

socialist of sorts. The State must do for the people what the people as wage-earners could never, evidently, do for themselves. The State must become schoolmaster, doctor, dentist, poor-man's guardian and the benefactor of old age. Everything, in short, which formerly had been the office of fatherhood. Men must elect their fathers, since those whom God had bestowed upon them were impotent.

And so, side by side, with the lowest-wage system grew up the system of public relief in all its forms. Public education and public medical services do not figure as "costs", except indirectly through the system of taxation. They do not, therefore, impose much of a handicap in the race for private-signature-money against black men and yellow men. They may even help to keep costs down by increasing the power to work. With ruthless hands family life was stripped of its dignity and independence and every man's child became the son or daughter of Old Mother Money Power, dressed up to look like a popularly elected government. The old lady supplied her children with the kind of knowledge it was good for them to receive, knowledge tinged with socialism on the one hand and "financialism" on the other.

"We go to work to get the money to buy the food to make us fit to go to work to get the money . . ."

Family life, in such circumstances, was apt to look rather uninviting. Fathers could buy nothing and mothers were slaves. Only the State seemed to possess resources and capacity.

But how quickly, if he got the chance, every man

separated himself from the benefits and joys of State supervision. The moment a working man made a bit of money he took his children away from the public elementary school and sent them to a private school. He ceased to employ "panel" doctors, too, or even to go in illness to voluntary hospitals. And why? Because it is the instinct of every man to make provision for his own children and because every man, in his heart, dislikes the idea that he is one of a herd in receipt of public charity. Family feelings are as real and as right as the profit motive, because it is through the family that a child comes, normally, to man's estate. It is true that poultry-farmers can hatch eggs in incubators and rear chicks in "feeders". It is also true that, in the absence of poultry-farmers, hens hatch their own eggs and rear their own chicks. If the object is the eating of the chicks the poultry-farmer is, no doubt, an excellent substitute for the hen. But if the object is the rearing of new hens and their equipment for the business of living the poultry-farmer is no substitute at all. The poultry-farmers in Whitehall and elsewhere reared masses of excellent "table poultry" for the Masters of Money, de-natured and demoralized boys and girls with their minds befogged and their instincts thwarted. Only money could secure escape from this system of farming. Where money was available, escape instantly took place.

Now, when money will be generally available, all will escape. Family life will be restored as naturally, as certainly and as universally as would occur upon the poultry-farm if the poultry possessed any freedom of choice. When men have wages, or other incomes, which are large enough to enable them to be the fathers of their children in the full sense of that word, fatherhood will be resumed throughout the world. Men will pay for education—such education as they desire—for doctors, dentists, games instructors and all other services. They will thus become, once more, the heads of their families and will recover their power to direct and guide the thoughts and actions of their children.

In consequence, respect for parents will increase side by side with the respect of women for their husbands and of men for their wives. The Englishman's home will become his castle once more and planners, controllers, bureaucrats and the whole army of interference will be warned off.

There will thus grow up a new generation very unlike that which is now in possession of the world. These young men and young women will possess health and wealth and be free in mind from the dreadful anxieties which bore upon their fathers and mothers. They will serve and love one another joyously . . . in the making of the profit of beautiful things. Those who doubt this may be urged to examine their own lives in order to discover how far the fear of poverty has influenced these lives away from hearts' desire, and how far the departure from hearts' desire has influenced health and happiness.

CHAPTER XIX

THE KING'S GRACE

THESE changes in the lives of men and women are bound to be reflected in the structure of states. At the present moment there exists throughout Europe the idea that a great struggle is going on between dictatorship and democracy upon the issue of which will depend the political and social future of mankind. In fact, as has been seen, both dictatorships and democracies have been engaged in a much greater struggle with a common enemy. They have been trying to wrest the means of livelihood from hands close fisted upon these means.

At the risk of repetition it must be insisted that the world crisis arose because America was following a course which threatened the Debt System. That system, in accordance with its habit when attacked, at once withdrew its money from the world, no doubt in the full expectation that America would soon capitulate. But America did not capitulate. The strangulation continued. The President of the United States, Mr. Roosevelt, found himself in consequence, when he took office, unable to obtain advances from the bankers. He attacked them, seized the entire stock of gold and by devaluing it, provided himself with £1,000,000,000.

He was now able to force the banks to accommodate him, especially as national feeling had been aroused to a pitch of enthusiasm by the New Deal and its Blue Eagle.

This strong action saved America and gave Europe an object lesson. One after the other, the European governments fanned the flames of patriotism; one after the other they extracted loans from reluctant bankers who dared not oppose them, unbalanced their budgets and engaged in schemes of public works. At the end only England was left, flattering herself that her budget remained "sound", but anxiously aware that she had defaulted on her War Debts to America.

Both democracy and dictatorship, therefore, forced the hands of the Money Power. Both brought so great a pressure to bear on the Masters of Money that these Masters found themselves compelled to fight for their power. The first battle, that of October 1934, ended indecisively, but in the second and much greater battle, which lasted from March 1st to June 6th, 1935, the Money Power was broken.

The power which belongs to money therefore has ceased, suddenly, to be international and has become national. In other words it has passed from a body of private persons operating in all countries to the government of each individual country. Want of money, in consequence, will not now break any government in the world for there is no national banking organization strong enough to refuse to accommodate its government. It follows that every political movement or structure which was based on the Debt System, whether in support of it or in opposition to it, will dwindle and disappear.

Among such institutions are political parties. The real difference between democracy and dictatorship, as seen recently in Europe, was a difference of method in resistance. All countries had the same master, the same need and the same difficulty. At the beginning of the World Crisis all countries, even Soviet Russia, were assured that Money would win. All, therefore, "lay low", murmured that "sound finance always pays" and waited to behold the immolation of the trans-Atlantic rebel. This attitude was common, in our own country, to each of the political parties, even to the Communist party. In the presence of the hawk the little birds did not dare even to twitter.

It is idle to call this sort of thing democracy. It was no more democracy than the Nazi Government or the Fascist Government or the Bolshevist Government, is democracy. It was crude dictatorship by an unseen master about whom only this was known that those who rebelled against his power were marked out for destruction and were, invariably, destroyed. There can be small doubt that, if Englishmen had known the truth about their democracy they would have exchanged it quite readily for an open and frank dictatorship. That might, at least, have been conducted and controlled by Englishmen or by an Englishman.

On the other hand the open dictatorships could not, in these early days of the crisis, offer their people anything better than was being offered by the hidden dictatorships in England and France. These open dictatorships, therefore, had other, secret dictatorships preying upon them. All were the servants of the same master no matter by what names they might choose to call themselves. All, equally, democracies and dictatorships, were penniless beggars upon the doorstep of Money. None could command a shilling for any purpose on earth.

But if the apparent differences were unreal there were, in fact, some real differences. A dictatorship, so long as its popularity lasts, is stronger than a system of parties because its organization more nearly resembles that of an army. Where there are parties, the one cancels the other out. A dictator, on the contrary, has invariably come to power by crushing all his opponents. He can, therefore, present to his enemies a united front and can bring a degree of pressure to bear upon them which cannot possibly be brought in a democracy. This was apparent, as has been seen, during the second stage of the crisis when it became obvious that America was not going to be beaten so easily as had been supposed. In France and England lip service continued to be paid on all occasions to the virtue of "sound finance" whereas in Germany and Italy bellicose speeches proclaimed to the Masters of Money that above money there is the nation.

It will, properly, be objected to this statement that America is a democracy. If resistance began and was continued in America, it ought to follow that democracy possesses qualities of strength which dictatorship does not possess. This point merits a very careful examination by all those who aspire to understand the political structure of the world into which we are entering.

The American Constitution differs from that of France or England in the respect that it embodies an office, the Presidency, which is, in essentials, an elective monarchy. The President of the United States is elected by the whole people to be their head and chief during a period of years and to exercise on their behalf what is, in effect, sovereign power. He is a king in all but the name, possessed of more real power that most of the European kings used to possess and answerable to nobody during his term of office.

There is all the difference in the world between this office and the office of Prime Minister in France or England. A Prime Minister is always a party leader. He is answerable, at all times, to Parliament as well as to his own party and he can, therefore, do nothing without first obtaining the consent of large numbers of persons. There will, invariably, be persons in his Parliament or Party who will make it their business to oppose "any tinkering with finance"—from the highest motives—and consequently monetary reform is virtually impossible to him.

But the President of the United States acts alone, in the full assurance that he has the majority of the people behind him. In Mr. Roosevelt's case the majority was overwhelming. A powerful sovereign, therefore, sat in the White House. America was a monarchical as opposed to a financial democracy. More closely than any other in the world her government system approximated to that of the European

Kingdoms in the Middle Ages where monarchies, elective and other, supplied the means of restraining the power and acquisitiveness of the barons.

Mr. Roosevelt has, throughout, behaved respectfully to Congress. But his seizure of the gold stocks, nevertheless, was a kingly act in the most exalted tradition of kingship. He spoke of it himself as a vindication of the national sovereignty and later, in his silver policy, actually re-introduced the word " Seignorage ", awakening it from its long mediæval slumber. Nor, in thus acting, was he taking a single step outside of the Constitution which he had promised to uphold. The American Constitution, as has been said, holds a niche for kings. Mr. Roosevelt's service consisted in the fact that he understood the constitution better than any of his predecessors and made use of it, for the people, as none, probably, of his predecessors had dared.

In other words it was neither democracy (as the term is understood in Europe) nor dictatorship but monarchy which flung down the challenge to Money and so put new courage into the hearts of all men. Because America had been a debtor country during the whole of the Nineteenth Century (and therefore of no importance) the Masters of Money had overlooked the fact that she retained, in its essential outlines, the only political institution which, at any period of history, had been able to withstand their attacks. At the most critical moment in their greatest struggle they found themselves faced with that mysterious power which, based solely upon consent, partakes nevertheless of the excellent virtue of fatherhood.

In saying this, however, sight must not be lost of the fact that the American President occupied a position such as no ruler in Europe has ever occupied. As has been said, he was virtually immune from foreign attack, and he possessed resources of so extensive and so varied a character that no pressure of economic isolation could cause him anxiety. These advantages would have been useless to a Prime Minister or a dictator. In the possession of a king they were the means of salvation.

History is a record of experiments in government. Those experiments which succeeded have, invariably, become the basis of future action. Thus, when Monarchy was defeated in the Seventeenth and Eighteenth Centuries by moneylending, armed with its new weapon of signature-money, the world turned away in pity or scorn from the bedraggled thrones. Now, however, that monarchy has defeated Money in a greater conflict than that which destroyed the Houses of Stuart and Bourbon, the world will come again to the King's house. Parties, bereft of those secret funds by which they have been sustained, will fall; dictatorships will become kingships or perish.

This is obvious when the fact is recalled that party labels furnish still another example of a shadow which has replaced its substance. The substance of political controversy is competition in administration, just as the substance of controversy among craftsmen is competition in the making of good profit. The shadow in both cases consists of an accountancy. Political accountancy is, properly, the prestige and power which come to great servants of the people so that their ability to serve may be increased and established. When accountancy becomes substance, the object of politicians is to obtain power and prestige, by any means. Just as the manufacturer produces shoddy in order to secure a money-profit so the political party makes its wild promises in order to secure " the sweets of office ". Thus profit and prestige are dragged forth from the goods and the service and set up as independent idols. The substance is eviscerated to make a shadow. Men worship figures and figments.

For this reason a deep contempt of party politics infects many honest minds. The game is so obvious; the prize, by comparison with the pains taken to secure it, so petty. Moreover, the whole apparatus of prize-getting is so absurd. There is, palpably, no such man as a Tory or a Liberal or a Socialist or a Communist. These are the labels not of men but of gangs greedy of prestige or power. Each of the gangs is supplied with its " party machine " and " caucus " and there is no room for any candidate, at any election, who has not bowed the knee, in the first instance, to one or other of the gang leaders. Gangs are always " financed " by somebody, they are never financed by wholly disinterested persons. Knowledge of these facts surrounds the party system with a fog of suspicion which makes Government an object not of honour and respect but of scorn.

This is the system which grew up upon the ruins of the old monarchical system and which must and will be cleared away now that its author and begetter, the

Debt System, is in process of dissolution. England is specially fortunate in that her Royal House remains to her. She is the more fortunate in that the occupant of her throne possesses the love and confidence of the whole people because, in years of selfless devotion to the people's good, he has won that love and confidence. It was the King who, in the anxious days of 1931, when the Masters of Money were demanding that "Doles" be cut to ribbons, travelled to London from Scotland in order to exercise his Royal prerogative and make the head of the fallen Labour Government his new Prime Minister. That was a gesture of hope to the poorest, a promise that such sacrifice as might be called for should be the sacrifice of all. Where others fainted, so that they would have acceded to every insolent and ruinous demand of Money, the King upheld the great dignity of his office before the world. He was father, then, to all his people and all his people recognized him and blessed him. There was manifestation, surely, of the hand of Almighty God in that Jubilee Procession which upon the sixth of May of this year passed through London Streets while the Masters of Money were reeling back, beaten already, from their great assault. Englishmen will rejoice in the days to come that the dying yells of the tiger were swallowed up in the cheers which greeted a sovereign and a friend.

CHAPTER XX

RESTORATION

MONARCHY, therefore, is a political institution *sui generis*. It owes nothing to any other kind of political institution. All other political institutions are secular; but monarchy is always religious.

It was this religious character of monarchy which endowed it, and which still endows it, with its strength. The King is the Shepherd; one of the Popes defined that " grace of God " whereby Kings reign as " the power to protect the sheep from the wolves ". Grace, in other words, was no mere embellishment of courtiers. It was lively truth, Kingship in action, an excellent protection.

A careful student of the American Constitution will discover that this idea of " grace " was present to the minds of those who framed the constitution. These men had experience of bad barons, leaders who had abused the privileges of leadership in order to devour the sheep. They saw that, in addition to its representatives, a people must possess a head, a man chosen because of his qualities of leadership, in whose person the whole nation might find a focus and a defender. They saw, too, that King and People constitute a very different political entity from Dictator and Party. There have been Kings who were party leaders, barons of barons; but such are not in the royal tradition of service and do not obey the "royal law". America's President, it was resolved, should be the chosen of all. In process of time the party system, in America as in Europe, swallowed up the Presidential office, so that presidents were nominated and elected on a party ticket. But the essential qualities remained for a great man to find and to exalt.

"Our Constitution," said Mr. Roosevelt in his inaugural address, "is so simple, so practical, that it is possible always to meet extraordinary needs by changes in emphasis and arrangement without loss of essential form."

Monarchy, in one form or another—for names matter nothing—will be restored throughout the world. That is to say there will, in each country, be an elected head of the people in whom will be vested, permanently or temporarily, the whole executive function. This ruler will be the chief of all the services of government and it will be his concern, by and with his people's love, to hold to their duty all the distinguished men who, by reason of their special abilities, have been placed in positions of trust. At the first sign of revolt on the part of any of these "notables", the ruler in the people's name will dispossess him of his office. Notables who have served well will be given additional privileges that they may be enabled to serve better. Notables will be elected by the people but will do homage, on appointment, to the ruler. All Members of Parliament will be chosen in this way.

The ruler himself will be sacred, in the true meaning of that word. He will be a man made holy and set apart, as living sacrifices were made holy and set apart. Thus, he will enshrine in his person the mystery of fatherhood, for the father is made the sacrifice for his family in that he is their protector unto death. Men put garlands of gold on Kings' heads and anointed Kings' brows with oil, for thus were sacrifices garlanded and anointed towards the burning. The King was the People's Man, their father, he who, if need be, was ready to be offered up on their behalf. There is much more, evidently, in such a conception than mere secular representation. Everywhere this leadership, be it called Presidency or Monarchy, touches the mysterious and the holy. So will it be always. For this man has been made lover as well as leader. The excellent mystery of love is proclaimed in his office.

Into the ruler's hands will pass the control of money, its issue and its regulation ; and this control will be the chief among his secular offices. At the first suggestion that a notable man is trying to tamper with the People's money or the People's level of prices, he will be deposed, arraigned and, if found guilty, most severely punished. Moneylending will thus be prevented. The Ruler will supervise also such public works as may be agreed upon, but, in general, there will be no production or trading by Government because every man will be free to offer to his neighbours such service as he may desire to offer and will be free, also, to derive such profit as he may be able to obtain. All notables, as has been said, will be elected ; all will be compelled to do homage before entering upon their duties. Nor will monopolies of any kind be tolerated—supposing that the monetary system should not in every instance destroy the power to acquire or hold monopolies.

It is probable that history will repeat itself and that men, having found a good ruler will surround him with the lively symbolism of rulership, thus making and calling him King. It is probable, too, that the King's office will again become hereditary because there are great and obvious advantages in a hereditary system which, as it may be argued, outweigh its evident dangers. Strong and good rulers cannot always be found; but it may be so contrived that the office, being fortified by its symbolism, shall carry a weaker man as if he was a stronger. The upholding of the King's office is the first duty and the most important duty of the people. Bad Kings must be ruthlessly driven from their thrones, for there can be no right of Kingship except that power of grace which is fatherhood and leadership in action.

It is instructive to note that, just as shadow replaced substance in wealth, in production and in politics, as the direct consequence of the rule of Money, so also in Kingship reality became obscured by its accountancy. The accountancy of Kings is the homage of their peoples. As children give themselves to their fathers and mothers from love and honour, so the peoples who have been greatly led and protected give themselves to their Kings. But if Kings declare that their royal blood is title to love and possession, they are seekers of power for its own sake, makers of money-profit, masters of a fraudulent accountancy. Hereditary right unsupported by any other claim is blood magic just as usury is the magic of the ledger.

All the contempt that has fallen upon Kings and nobles and upon those who create profit has its source and origin in the absurdities to which, by one means or another, the Masters of Money have contrived to wed those institutions and activities which are most likely to offer them battle. Thus were men stripped of all means of defending themselves and made enemies of that order of thinking by which alone their salvation might have been accomplished.

A generation less closely in touch with the horror of the Debt System will derive amusement, certainly, from consideration of the slogans and watchwords by which the political structure of that system was supported. How, for example, can men be held in equality if they are free or granted liberty if equality is the object of government? How can the people possess the "power of the purse" if they must borrow private signatures in order to live? How can there be "no taxation without representation" in a world in which banks are free to expand credit and so to diminish the buying-power of everybody's money? Again, how can a political party represent the people when half or nearly half of the people have voted against it?

CHAPTER XXI

FLESH AND FIGURES

THE most abused word in our language is the word sacrifice, for its meaning has been changed out of recognition and its latter meaning set in opposition to its former. As we understand the word to-day it signifies surrender, whether of goods, of joy or of life, and there is conveyed, also, the suggestion that such surrender is merit, in itself and of itself, of the very highest order.

This was not at all what the original users of the word meant to convey. For them sacrifice meant to make holy or sacred; as has been pointed out above, a sacred person was a person set apart. Thus by self-sacrifice was understood the kind of dedication which an artist makes when he spends his faculties of spirit and mind in the creation of a picture—a joyous self-forgetfulness, an ecstasy of giving forth unto life, a creation—matter therefore of song and dance, of garlands and feasting.

Every man made such sacrifice in an age when all men plied a craft, and there was neither sentimentality nor sorrow about it. These old craftsmen, indeed, would have rubbed their eyes at the idea that they must strangle their native impulses in order to do good to their neighbour or make prigs or martyrs of themselves in order to love him. They knew how to love their neighbours and do them good, or at any rate they knew by what means a sense of neighbourly kindness could be experienced. One had only to make something, profitably, and one's heart would glow with happiness and goodwill.

And why? Probably they could not have answered such a question because they were not thinking people, given to self-analysis, but doing and feeling people, given sometimes to mirth. Possibly the joy came in at one's fingers while one's fingers touched wood or stone or paint or fabric. Like a mother's joy in the touching of her babe. Possibly at one's eyes in the regard of curves and lines and the meeting-places and clashes and reconciliations, the tensions and the resolutions of tension of these two. Like a man's joy of a young horse. How should they know whence the joy came? Or the quality of it? They had received it without weighing or measuring or dissection.

No beating of the air, here, to make the wind howl. No Puritan's long face or sufferer's glances. Why be sad when you can create something? Why humbug your neighbour when you can supply him with goods. Why hurt yourself to please God when you can make toys for children or give them fruit or sweets or a lift on your back. In fine, why talk when you can do, think when you can feel, be sentimental when you can help?

But what if one may do nothing, make nothing, be of help to none? What if between hands and materials there is a gulf set so that the world is a museum full of prohibitions to touch? How then shall a man love God or his neighbour? Can he set himself apart in such circumstances, or sing or dance or make merry? Can he forget himself and, in forgetfulness, fill his lungs with gladness? Surely he will be prisoner of his frustration, martyr of his uselessness.

The self-sacrifice, of which so much is spoken to-day, is a name for nothing. As if a father can best serve his children by drowning himself or blowing out his brains. It is sign and index of our exile in the Far Country that we have substituted immolation for service, exalting the one and despising the other. Thus, indeed, have we fitted ourselves with a religious and philosophical basis for the wizardries of our economics and our statesmanship.

The religion of the Debt System indeed, forms an essential foundation for that system, without which the system could scarcely have been established and could not have endured. It is a religion in which science and magic are blended so skilfully that few have penetrated to the underlying absurdity. Briefly, it is the religion of the symbol made alive. The priests of Debt make spirit and flesh of their numerals. Figures become wealth; figures become the profitable bounty of nature and of art; figures become the homage of peoples, their love and their fealty. But even that was not enough. It was necessary that this corruption of magic should ascend also to the Throne of the Heavenly Grace, setting the ledger, with its record of debt, higher than Love. The accountancy of Love is worship.

But Love which calculates, Love which gives not Himself is not worshipped except out of fear.

When the Christian Church abandoned the position of the Canonists and made weak its prohibition of moneylending it denied, by implication, the brotherhood of men. For a brother cannot use his brother's misfortune to make money out of him. To deny the brotherhood of men is to deny, also, the Fatherhood of God, a truth which was present to the mind of St. Thomas Aquinas. In consequence, the priests of Debt were able, under the Christian cloak, to present the world with a new god, he whose mills grind slowly but exceeding small, like the mills of usury. Debt became god as debt had become the King, the artist, the craftsman, the husbandman, even wealth itself.

The way was open, now, for a transformation of the Christian religion into a supernatural banking transaction with its instruments of credit and its cancelled overdrafts. That grotesquerie, as had been foreseen, could not long survive among rational men and consequently schism after schism divided the Church amid burnings and torturings and dreadful exhibitions of malice. Men turned from the god whom their hearts rejected to seek new gods. They found Chance, Fate, the inscrutable forces of Nature, and the priests of Debt, guiding their thoughts, showed them " the law of the jungle ", the survival of the fittest.

No need now to pay even lip service to Christianity. Life had come, as the ownership of debt had come, by accident of fitness. By struggle and violence and the trampling under of opponents. Here was science to be guide through all the labyrinthine jungle, from that " primæval sludge ", that secular mud, wherein once upon a time, but once only, inflamed molecules of hydrogen and carbon and nitrogen and oxygen—perhaps sulphur too—held congress, one with another, and produced a living cell. Had there been a God He might have known how it happened. But there was the fact, with science to attest it. The cell divided. There were two cells; debtor and creditor perhaps.

In any case there was no God, no author, no begetter. Man had no ancestors except hydrogen and carbon and nitrogen and oxygen, perhaps sulphur. And no law except the survival of the fittest. All men, therefore, were self-made. All were more fit or less fit, creditors or debtors, and civilization consisted in creditors refraining from killing their debtors too soon. Creditors were men like gods because they could make trees bear fruit and cattle bear young and money breed. They could fertilize deserts, too, with figures and of the same figures create life upon the earth. The sun and the early and the latter rain were in their hands; thunderbolts also. By them kings reigned and princes decreed judgment. Not a sparrow but was reckoned in their accountancy.

Who could doubt it? The price-level surged up and the desert was red with blossom. Men went forth to the fields and the harvests were gathered. There was clang of hammers in a million workshops. Blossoms, too, in children's cheeks and laughter in their mouths. The price-level sank down and the grass withered. Fear fell upon the habitations of men and there was silence over the land. The silence of little children. . . .

How real it all was! How free from sentiment and illusion! Accountancy. Accountancy. Accountancy. The unanswerable logic of figures. The testament of test-tubes and balances. Measurement. Experiment. That only is true which works. Who are we to be beguiled with old wives' fables? Do we not possess the wisdom of ages? Can we not measure the stars, weigh the electron, ride upon the storm? Are not the secrets of life and of death our secrets? Who is god but man? Who among men is god but the money-lender by whom scientists think and engineers plan great marvels? On and up. Evolution through loans. Progress. Perfectibility.

And what now that the level of prices may not be moved up or down? Who will make harvest now for hungry mouths? By whom shall the trees bear fruit and the cattle bring forth their young? Can England, can Europe, can the world support their populations in the absence of the fertilizing figures? The gods depart and they have left us no other gods. . . .

Men, in the days to come, will not forsake science, which has bestowed excellent gifts upon them. On the contrary they will, in all probability, return, under her guidance to the ancient truths. For there is no more conspicuous or astonishing trait of the philosophy of the age of Debt than its obstinate refusal to take observed fact into consideration. There was, it is true, a veneer of science; but under the veneer lay frank magic. And the magic was much stronger than the science.

It is a fundamental rule of biology, for example, that

life can proceed only from life. That rule was enunciated by Pasteur who proved it by numberless experiments and gave it to the world at the great demonstration at the Sorbonne which was attended by Napoleon III, his Empress, and most of his Court. Pasteur displayed two flasks containing clear soup. One of these had been sealed, while boiling, some years earlier. The other, which had been filled the day before, had not been sealed. The soup in the sealed flask was clear; that in the unsealed flask was already turbid. Pasteur invited his audience to ask themselves why, during so long a period of time, the contents of the sealed flask had remained undeteriorated. He answered the question by saying that life had been excluded. There was no sign of life in the sealed flask because life does not arise spontaneously out of material things but only from creatures already alive.

This doctrine is now held as an article of faith by every biologist in the world and there is not left any biologist who supposes that life can arise through some accident of chemical or physical combination. That being so, it is pertinent to inquire if any special manifestations attend, usually, the proceeding of one life out of another. When a unicellular organism is about to divide, and so to reproduce itself, well-known but very remarkable changes occur in the structure of the nucleus, that nerve-centre or life-centre of the cell. These changes display a rearrangement of certain lively elements to which the name chromosomes has been given. The cell seems to become more actively alive. The chromosome pattern is outspread, spindle-like. Nucleus is born from nucleus; substance, like swarming bees, attaches itself to the new centre and moves with it into separate and independent form. The two cells come out again, as it were, from their ecstasy.

Compare this picture with the mating of the queen bee—high up, within the summer light, when he who wins her will pay, on the instant, with his life. Or with the mad rush of the silver eel to the sea that it may go back, whence it came, to spawn and die in deepest water of the Atlantic. Or with the belling of stags as they come by night to their death-fights for the hinds. Compare it with the desperate courage of a mother hedge-sparrow as she covers her nest from hawk or crow. With the swift resolution of the man or woman who plunges into fire to save son or daughter.

All these, by some alchemy, have been changed so that Nature herself seems to have forsaken them. Once they were timid, careful, self-preserving and protecting, alert for sight or sound of danger, ready to lay the whip upon every faculty—to win escape. But now ecstasy of boldness has cast out fear. All are sacrificed, made holy, set apart. They wear garlands of light and colour. And their joy breaks forth so that the woods are filled with music and the world is full of mirth.

It is ecstasy, abandon, sacrifice. It is the death of self and the resurrection from the dead. The process of being born again. And out of the process, proceeding with song and dance, creation, the coming of life from life, the transmutation of ecstasy into flesh.

Thus, and thus only, is life created. Thus, and thus only, can material things be caught up into the whirlwind of life. If the word be not made flesh, there is no flesh. So that flesh is the witness of the word, of the ecstasy, of the sacrifice. Witness that its maker put self away; died and in great joy rose again from the dead. And this witness is true. Let men open their eyes.

Let them use reason, too, in the service of science. There is a law of science that a man may argue only from the known to the unknown. Those, therefore, who would seek in Creation knowledge of the Creator must abjure the primæval sludge. The flesh is witness, not of concatenations of the chemical elements, but of the Word. Of the ecstasy, of the joy of resurrection, of the sacrifice. Science, therefore, may find no God but Love. No God but a Being, ecstatic, filling the Heavens with His glory and great joy. No God but He out of Whom the Word, proceeding, is made flesh. No God but He Who in timeless habitation as upon the earth has become Sacrifice, died, risen again from the dead.

It is the faith of all things created. Humanity, above all creatures, is witness of God's Love, of God's Death, of God's Resurrection. If men be set free they will bear that witness, daily, throughout life, in the family, in the workshop, in the parliament house. Fathers and mothers will bear witness. Brothers and sisters. Neighbours. Craftsmen, too, of their ecstasy of touch and sight, artists, musicians, poets, men of science, physicians. The King, garlanded and anointed, upon his throne, making of his "King-thought" a nation.

Nor is this most holy procession of the Word static, a unity. Love in action cannot be unity but must be Trinity because, ever, there is the Lover, His Love (the Word) and His Comfort. All this truth, certainly, is hidden in the hearts of men. It will emerge, now, out of their hearts to give them back again that sense of mystery which the moneylenders' magic corrupted and destroyed. With eyes set upon the law of the survival of the most loving they will come again, through science, to the Revelation of Him Who testified: "I am the Resurrection and the Life."

And so Europe will resume her faith and Christendom be rebuilt in the hearts of men.

CONCLUSION

CHAPTER XXII

THE LOST CIVILIZATION

It is frequently asserted that civilizations, like men, have their youth and their hey-day and their old age. There are numerous instances with which this assertion is supported, for example, the civilizations of Egypt, of Greece and of Rome. It is usual, however, to omit the most conspicuous example of them all—namely, the civilization of Europe.

The reason, of course, is that it is not generally admitted that European civilization has perished. On the contrary, historians profess to see an evolution from the Dark Ages to the Middle Ages, and so onwards to these latter days. They call it the march of liberty, of representative institutions, of enlightenment. Do not Magna Charta and the Petition of Rights exist to prove the case—to say nothing about the Declaration of the Rights of Man?

The differences, however, which exist between conditions of life in, say, the Thirteenth Century and the Nineteenth Century place great obstacles in the way of acceptance of continuity. For one thing the avowed objects of living differed completely in the two periods. For another, the political and economic systems were built upon entirely different foundations. Finally there has continued, since the Fourteenth Century, opposition, more or less feeble, to the system which, in that century, obtained the support of the majority of Europeans.

This opposition, indeed, is the real continuity, a civilization within a civilization, always conquered and yet always coming again, somehow, somewhere, to challenge the legitimacy of its supplanter, until, at the last, the supplanter has been compelled to make terms.

What is called the history of democracy furnishes many examples of this guerrilla warfare. When the Masters of Money stood at the height of their power democracy was held in contempt. "Sheep make poor shepherds." But when difficulties with Big Business began to arise, the value of a rival party to that of the great industrialists began to be understood. Money then became available to support Socialism and, later, Communism. So far as England was concerned, however, the effect was not at all what had been expected. Englishmen displayed a great reluctance to be enlisted in revolutionary movements and a great eagerness to restore the lost heritage of the "good old days". Thus, the Labour movement became a mouthpiece of ideas that were essentially feudal and English Socialism moved in the direction of the mediæval guilds. This was not to the liking of the Money Power which has continued, at intervals, to try to inject Marxian doctrines into our left-wing parties. These doctrines make no headway. The mass of the English people is Christian-minded, monarchical in feeling and individualistic. Englishmen reject instinctively such devices as "rationalization" and planned economy and continue to hanker for the day when they will be able to rid themselves for ever of class consciousness in all its forms.

Nor is this reactionary spirit confined to England. It has been necessary to organize the "proletariat" as an army in order to induce men to have anything to do with the proletariat. Armies have rank but no class. Thanks to the lost civilization, Europeans do not believe and cannot be made to believe, that there is one flesh of landowners, and another of merchants and another of labourers. Thus the attempts to divide and rule have very often produced union instead of division—the Fascist and Nazi movements are examples in point. Both profess democratic principles. Both have adopted feudal methods. Both have enlisted the "proletariat" against the Masters of Money. Both may, quite easily, assume the monarchical form at any moment.

European civilization, in other words, is showing a reaction to the passage of time quite different from that displayed by the ancient civilizations. European civilization was dead and is alive again. It was stricken down, in full activity, by a conjuring trick of money against which it possessed no weapons of defence, and that blow was represented, during centuries, as a great liberation whereby civilization had been purged of its errors. But in their hearts men knew that it was not so. They knew that the so-called progress had cost them their common lands, their yeomen's rights, their holy days, their dignity as men and Christians. And they guessed that those who should have been the guardians and upholders of civilization had deserted and gone over to the enemy. The spectacle of notables in *full possession* of the land was not misunderstood. There were some in every generation, who recognized the act of pillage for what it was and who remained unimpressed by the assertions that the seizure of the property of Mother Church by the baronage had enriched the English and other European peoples. It was easy to lead such disgruntled folk against kings and nobles who had, so palpably, failed of their duty ; but it was not easy to convince them that plutocracy is a good exchange for a high-souled leadership.

More and more, therefore, the Money Power hid itself in mists of economic jargon which ordinary people could never hope to understand. Even the kings, while they still wielded power, had been at a loss to understand it and to know where all the wealth that the moneylenders appeared to possess had come from. How little they guessed that it had not come from anywhere and did not anywhere exist ! Imagine the rage into which Henry VIII must have fallen had he realized that the gold which he had ravished from the tombs of the saints, in order to obtain the means of carrying on his government, was being exchanged for nothing more substantial than "promises to pay". Henry VIII seized the treasure of the English Church ; but he died a bankrupt. Queen Elizabeth was bankrupt throughout practically the whole period of her reign—in spite of the Spanish gold. And so it went on, from dynasty to dynasty. The debts easily outran the income because the invention of private-signature-money had conferred control of the price-level. The old civilization was nibbled at by millions of rats from all the sewers of West and East.

But not consumed. There are things which even rats cannot kill, and the European spirit is one of them. European civilization, therefore, survived the plague. What the world is about to enjoy is not a new civilization in the sense that no precedent exists, but an old and tried civilization which during more than 1,000 years was the basis of life throughout the West. It is astonishing how little is known about this civilization ; not less astonishing is the volume of the propaganda, the object of which, apparently, was to suggest that the lost civilization was a very bad one and that mankind was well rid of it. But, as has been said, the cathedrals and great secular buildings exist to cast doubt upon this propaganda. It will scarcely be contended that the minds which conceived Westminster Abbey, Canterbury Cathedral, York Minster, Ripon Cathedral, Wells Cathedral, Ely Cathedral, the cathedrals at Lincoln and Peterborough, were sunk in spiritual darkness or of a texture coarser than the minds which built the power station in Lots Road, Chelsea, or the Albert Hall or Olympia. Again, Guildhall is not a building which compares unfavourably with the County Hall at Westminster, nor are the buildings which surround the Grand Place in Brussels inferior to those which adorn the neighbouring heights. Indeed, it is obvious that these older buildings, religious and secular alike, proceeded from minds in ecstasy and expressed a lively sense of the joy and importance of life. There was the secret of the lost civilization. Its basis was belief in the transcendant importance of the individual as a living and immortal soul. It was upheld by pillars of human dignity. It was nourished by an all-pervading sense of the supernatural. *Lux in tenebris.* Within the shrine there was passion of filtered ray and blended colour, moving upon the austere loveliness of the grey stone and the fretted wood; without were gargoyles and shapes of night. The picture of Everyman's soul. The demons flapped down to defile the sanctuary and the gloom of their wings extinguished light. Passion of love became passion of fear and hate—fear lest a man might lack bread for his children, hate against all others, his rivals in the eating of bread. You cannot have "costs systems" and cathedrals in the same world. Men become "hands" and are denatured. Everyman's soul is lost in the encircling gloom.

In the days that are near the sense of the supernatural will come back to men. Not a horrid magic of witchcraft and ghostcraft but that mystery which, like light, glows about the face of Love. We shall dare, once again, to read our Symbols because shadow and substance will be reconciled. We shall dare to think, not in fever as men without hope, about to die, but in genial leisure of the heirs of eternal life. Since flesh is witness of the Word, it is witness also of immortality. For there is a succession of ecstasy, from one generation to another, the Word made flesh;

flesh transmuted to the Word—this fervent and heroic flesh which will go into the fire or into the water for the Word's sake.

It is difficult for men and women who have been able to see no object in life except material gain to tolerate the idea of a personal immortality. For those who have lived close to nature and to her unfainting testimony, the idea is as easy and natural as breathing or sleeping. It is the men on the soil and the men upon the sea who have rescued the lost civilization and who will re-shape it in the days to come—those common people who, in all ages, have continued to hear Him gladly.

They are not fools and dolts, these simple-minded men and women. Nor restless like townspeople with the restlessness of exhaustion. They will not seek to throw away knowledge or dispense with the apparatus which knowledge has given. They do not fear science as townsmen fear her. Their world, therefore, will be new in the sense that, as has been said, they will remodel it in almost every detail. Houses, roads, means of communication—all will be changed. Great cities will melt that men may have room for their elbows. The cities that are to come will be centres not of commerce but of culture. In every home, too, there will be machines, improved hands and feet, with their gift of leisure time—aeroplanes, cars, electric machines, machines for making heat and machines for making cold, transmission machines to bring sight and sound of great events and open men's hearts to one another.

We have these already to some extent, because

science has marched ever against Poverty and Debt, and only very dull folk regret them. By the machines, in some sort, we have been set free. It was the gift of wireless, for example, which enabled Mr. Roosevelt to keep in touch with his farmers over the heads of the bankers' press and so to defeat that press. Never again can opinion be poured in single channels. There are too many wave-lengths and aeroplanes and motor-cars for that. The machines, again by displacing labour, have brought crisis to the knowledge and experience of all and so made it possible to organize resistance. The leisure they offer may seem a dangerous gift to men unaccustomed to leisure, but it would not so have appeared to those who, as in the Thirteenth Century, only worked during 200 days of the year. These men of the Middle Ages would not have been afraid because the necessity of work was reduced to a period of 100 days or 50 days or even seven days. They knew how to fill leisure with the tasks which cannot be performed quickly, in a hurry.

We shall regain that lost knowledge. There is so much to do in the world to-day, in order that the dirt and ruin of the Age of Debt may be cleared away, that none need fear too much idleness for his neighbour. Leisure will come slowly, when that necessary work is done. The present generation will have passed by then. Our children, free to follow their own bent, without benefit of busybody or planner, will not faint because all ways are wide open to them—even the way of contemplation in which there is no movement that secular eye can detect.

CHAPTER XXIII

NATION WITH NATION

It remains only to ask how far the international structure which existed seven centuries ago is likely to be reproduced in the days to come. Will nations tend to lose their identity? Will the dream of the United States of Europe be realized.

There have, in fact, been only three great "internationals" in Western history—namely, Imperial Rome, Christendom and Money. Each of these replaced the one before it. The presumption must lie, therefore, that a fourth international is now on the way. Further it seems probable that this fourth international will bear resemblance to the second out of which the last civilization directly proceeded. Are we to look, therefore, for a new Christendom?

Mr. Roosevelt said, in his address to the Federal Council of the Churches of Christ in America on December 6th, 1934:

> This new generation of ours . . . may not be as ready as were their fathers and mothers to accept the outward requirements or even many of the ancient observances of the several churches, yet I truly believe that these same churches can find in them a stronger support for the fundamentals of social betterment than many of the older generation are willing to concede.

The younger generation is not satisfied with the exposure of those in high places who seek to line their own nests with other people's money, to cheat their government of its just dues or to break the spirit of the law while observing its legalistic letter. This new generation seeks action—action by collective government and by individual education—toward the ending of practices such as these.

From the bottom of my heart I believe that this beloved country of ours is entering upon a time of great gain. That gain can well include a greater material prosperity, if we take care that it is a prosperity for a hundred and twenty million human beings and not a prosperity for the top of the pyramid alone. It can be a prosperity built on spiritual and social values rather than on special privilege and special power.

Towards that new definition of prosperity the churches and the governments, while wholly separate in their functioning, can work hand in hand. Government can ask the churches to stress in their teaching the ideals of social justice while, at the same time, government guarantees to the churches—Gentile and Jew—the right to worship God in their own way. The churches, while they remain wholly free from even the suggestion of interference in government, can at the same time teach their millions of followers that they have the right to demand of the government of their own choosing the maintenance and furtherance of "a more abundant life". State and Church are rightly united in a common aim. With the help of God we are on the road toward it.

The coming of the new international spirit, however, will in no sense diminish that elusive quality known as patriotism. Nations will not disappear but, on the contrary, are likely to grow more self-conscious. Nothing is more remarkable than the failure of modern writers either to define or to destroy the idea of a nation. The idea, indeed, seems to grow stronger the more fiercely it is attacked. What is a nation? Few can say and those who attempt to say are greatly daring because it is so easy to controvert them. But the fact remains. It remains, too, one of those facts for which men are willing to shed their blood.

It may be that nationhood constitutes a means of expression of the special qualities of which all of us are instinctively aware. Mr. John Smith of the town of Barnard Castle in the North Riding of Yorkshire loses nothing and gains much from the fact that he is, also, an Englishman and a Briton. His being a Briton does not in the least detract from his being an Englishman, and that, again, does not detract from his qualities of Yorkshireman, man of the North Riding, Barnard Castle man and member of the family of Smith. Each quality, indeed, fulfils the other, so that, by the time he is an Englishman, this good fellow possesses a great number of ways of making contact with other men and so of enriching the sum of human experience. Mr. Smith will not, probably, be averse from becoming also, and further, a European. But this new synthesis of his qualities will enlarge rather than diminish every one of them, making of him more and not less of a Briton, an Englishman, a Yorkshireman, a man of the North Riding, a Barnard Castle man and a Smith. It is upon convicts that numbers are bestowed. Men seek distinction, not the obliteration of distinctions. One of the most marked differences between the Roman Empire and Christendom lay in the Roman citizenship on the one hand and in the National Churches, loosely united together, on the other. It is the sword which unites. And in this respect money and the sword follow the same method. The Masters of Money were always the strongest opponents of " nationalism " and its most bitter critics. Their minions did not cease to pour scorn on the conception of an Englishman, a Frenchman, a German. Where, they demanded, are these strange creatures ? That propaganda was not conducted without an object. If a tyrant ruled in England Mr. Smith of Barnard Castle would be more and not less free because he was a Yorkshireman and a man of the North Riding, a Barnard Castle man and a Smith. If he were merely Englishman No. 10,000 or European No. 1,000,000 his chances of retaining any right at all would be worth nothing. It is the fervour of nationalism, as has been seen, which has defeated Money and saved the world.

Nationhood, indeed, like membership of a family, is a contact between man and Mother Earth. The " sacred soil " is no figment. Men who lose such contacts lose qualities of the soul. They are like craftsmen from whom the materials of their craft have been taken away. Unemployed persons in the spiritual sense. Prisoners of' their frustration. There is a national spirit to which men contribute and from which they take. A worthy spirit which equips those who partake of it for international contacts, just as the family spirit equips every member of the family for the contacts of the village and the county and the fatherland. Free peoples will not make surrender of this heritage.

The Fourth International, therefore, will be a free association of nations and not a union. It will find its basis of association in spiritual as opposed to political qualities. Thus the cultural inheritance of Europe will become, once more, the property of all her peoples as it was in the days when Gothic architecture and ornament carried their message to every heart. And the inheritance will grow and be enriched by each nation in its own way, from one generation to another.

THE END

For Product Safety Concerns and Information please contact our EU representative GPSR@taylorandfrancis.com Taylor & Francis Verlag GmbH, Kaufingerstraße 24, 80331 München, Germany